RENEWING THE SOCIAL STUDIES CURRICULUM

Walter C. Parker

Association for Supervision and Curriculum Development
Alexandria, Virginia

Acknowledgments

I have been fortunate to work with local social studies curriculum committees across the nation—in urban, suburban, and rural school districts. To them I offer my thanks. Their caring work and the practical intelligence they display in the face of the social upheavals that are shaking our schools continue to inspire me. Their efforts are especially noble because they are expected to do far more than the schools *can* do, because elected officials have done so little to help, and because so many education fads blithely ignore curriculum matters.

The members of these committees, along with my colleagues at the University of Washington and in Seattle area school districts, push me continually to rethink my notions of curriculum renewal in social studies. For this, I am especially grateful to Jim Banks, Pam Grossman, Elaine Aoki, and Ted Kaltsounis.

—Walter Parker
Associate Professor of Education
University of Washington, Seattle

Copyright © 1991 by the Association for Supervision and Curriculum Development, 1250 N. Pitt St., Alexandria, VA 22314, (703) 549-9110.

Printed in the United States of America.
Typeset by Valerie Sprague
Printed by Banta
Cover design by Weber Design

Ronald S. Brandt, *Executive Editor*
Nancy Modrak, *Managing Editor, Books*
Ginger R. Miller, *Associate Editor*
Stephanie Kenworthy, *Manager of Production*

Price: $13.95
ASCD Stock Number: B9102

Cover map © Diagram Visual Information, Ltd. Reprinted with permission.

Library of Congress Cataloging-in-Publication Data

Parker, Walter.
  Renewing the social studies curriculum/Walter C. Parker,
    p.   cm.
  Includes bibliographical references.
  ISBN 0-87120-177-1 : $13.95.
  1. Social studies—Study and teaching (Elementary)—United States.
  2. Social studies—Study and teaching (Secondary)—United States.
  3. Curriculum planning—United States.   I. Title.
LB1584.P28   1991   91-7655
300'.71'73—dc20   CIP

Renewing the Social Studies Curriculum

Foreword

IT'S NO SECRET THAT OUR NATION'S YOUNG PEOPLE ARE SORELY LACKING IN their historical and geographical knowledge of the world and even their country's role in it. For most of my school years I hated history. To me, it was merely a set of isolated facts to memorize with absolutely no relation to my life. Unfortunately, suffering through boring, seemingly irrelevant history classes is an experience shared by many students in the United States. The result is very little learning.

Many commissions and scholars have devised policy-level solutions to correct this situation. Yet none have dealt with the real reasons for the condition nor produced solutions that need no translation for grassroots implementation. *Renewing the Social Studies Curriculum* does.

In this book, Walter Parker suggests that the curriculum renewal process should be considered an opportunity to improve both teaching and learning in the social studies. Believing that students have a greater chance of learning that which they are taught, Parker concludes that our students do poorly in social studies partly because it often goes untaught--for a variety of reasons. He steps up to the reality that our social studies staffs and even our schools' missions too often take a back seat to sports and coaching qualifications.

Parker gives credence to the notion that "less is more" by emphasizing the need to establish essential learnings and provide students with sustained examination of a limited number of topics. He suggests making teachers a part of social studies curriculum improvement by giving them accurate content information and asking them how they would infuse it into their classrooms. He also encourages us to accept his challenge to align the written and taught curriculums, and he recommends using the "ideal" curriculum as a jumping off place for curriculum renewal.

Readers will find some real treasure nuggets in this text. Key to turning those nuggets into a fortune for social studies students are teachers who are involved in the curriculum renewal process; the availability of accurate, relevant content; methods for providing students with conceptual frameworks on which to hang information; and opportunities for students to apply their learning in familiar and unfamiliar settings and to experience authentic assessment.

DONNA JEAN CARTER
ASCD President, 1990-1991

iv

Introduction

THIS BOOK IS NOT ANOTHER REFORM PROPOSAL WRITTEN IN RESPONSE
to the widespread concern over students' poor showing on
standardized test scores in the United States. While the concern is
real and the low test scores sorely disappointing, the reform
proposals deserve the reader's keenest skepticism. Many are sharply
conservative documents distorted by nostalgic longing for simpler
days and by ignorance of decades of curriculum scholarship.

Here, no reform package is proposed. Rather, my focus is the art
of local social studies curriculum deliberation. Hence, it is a book
about the possibility of home-grown curriculum reform.
Home-grown? By this I mean the sort of reform that comes from the
hearts and minds of people who actually work with children in the
schools and on whose shoulders the burden of implementation lies.
Deliberation? Indeed. An appreciation of curriculum renewal as
deliberation reminds us that judgment, practical experience, study,
and conversation, not doctrine, are the core of this activity. Art?
Unquestionably. An appreciation of art in curriculum renewal
nudges planners toward issues of quality, meaning, and sensibility.
Art asks us to refine our "eye" so that we might sculpt a curriculum
in which we can take deep satisfaction. Without art and the
satisfaction it brings, curriculum planning easily becomes one more
bureaucratic ritual—tasks, meetings, flowcharts, and timelines;
motion masquerading as improvement. In this book, I apply the
curriculum arts to considerations of planning and assessing learning
in the social studies.

What Is Social Studies?

Social studies is that part of the kindergarten through 12th grade
school curriculum concerned particularly with history, geography,
and civics. We can integrate history and geography organically,

without fancy footwork, by including mapwork in every history lesson. We can create civics as *strong* civics when knowledge and actual civic participation are combined in what has been called participatory democracy or participatory citizenship.

Participatory citizenship, then, is a two-sided coin. To be sure, it has a vast and messy knowledge base. Participation without knowledge, action without understanding, obviously is folly. There is much to be learned, for example, about the institutions and conditions that sustain democracy and about what happens when they are absent or weak; about life in Asia, Africa, and Latin America; and about the economic development crisis facing the international system today.

On the participatory side, social and political life under the democratic ideal require that citizens and public officials share the labor-intensive work of making public policy. A proper education for participation, and one that is well within the reach of the social studies curriculum at every grade, emphasizes learning to participate in public discussions of the public's problems.

Discussion (talk, conversation, deliberation) is the most basic and essential form of participatory citizenship. It is in discussion that disagreements are revealed, clarified, and analyzed; alternatives created and explored; the notion of the "loyal opposition" made real; common purposes perceived; decisions made; and action planned. Talk is *not* cheap. In a very real sense, public talk is the medium through which the public is created. Consider only the sweeping changes in the Soviet Union where glastnost unleashed public talk and, hence, a new public.

Curriculum Renewal

Many of us are chagrined that students are not learning well history, geography, or civics—either strong or weak. Is it that they are not trying hard enough? This is of course a major cause, and there are all sorts of reasons for it, many beyond the control of educators. Has parental support for school success waned? This, we know, is a factor. Is instruction of poor quality? This is another part of the equation. But a fundamental cause, and one well within our control, is this: These subjects are not necessarily *taught*. If educational research can tell us anything, it is that students are more likely to learn something at school if it is taught than if it is not.

If students have not developed important knowledge, then we as curriculum planners must first ask where in the curriculum students are helped to learn it. If they cannot point to China or South Africa on a blank map of the world, we must ask where in the curriculum students are taught the locations of nations, where they practice identifying them on unlabeled world maps, and where they are held accountable. If students cannot tell us who the Nazis were, what they did, and what conditions supported their rise to power, we must ask where in the curriculum students are taught this material and where they are held accountable for knowing it. If they cannot describe the cultural diversity of North America today, explain how it got that way, and predict it for the next several decades, we must ask where in the curriculum they are taught this material and where they are held accountable. If students cannot write a decent analysis of a public issue, weighing the arguments, drawing historical parallels, taking a stand and supporting it, we must ask where in the curriculum they are taught to do these things, where they develop them, and where they are held accountable.

The primary task of any social studies curriculum renewal committee is to assure that important subject matter is taught—regularly, every day, in every grade, K-12. This involves essentially three matters for deliberation: judging the existing curriculum, both the written version and the one that actually is taught; making whatever changes are needed; and specifying the demonstrations of achievement that are expected from students at key points in their school progress.

An Overview

Chapter 1, "Challenging Lessons on Essential Learnings," briefly defines the major commitments of the book: planning a thought-provoking social studies curriculum, concentrating instruction time on a limited number of core learnings, and doing this within a demonstrable and readily apparent commitment to education for democratic character.

Chapter 2, "Contexts of Renewal," puts curriculum planning into its various social settings: school organization, community, and the difficult, nearly overwhelming, times in which we work as educators.

Chapter 3, "Deliberation for Change," presents a case study of curriculum deliberation by a district social studies curriculum planning committee. Analysis of the case introduces a number of issues and four "commonplaces" that should be kept in mind as curriculum planning proceeds: students, teachers, subject matters, and milieux.

Chapter 4, "Renewal Principles and Procedures," presents three general principles to guide curriculum renewal in social studies and an eight-part renewal model. Skipping around is encouraged and pitfalls are noted.

Chapter 5, "Goals, Issues, and Trends," gives an overview of social studies in the United States today. Drawing on data gathered over the past decade, we consider national curriculum patterns, alternatives, issues, and trends.

Chapter 6, "Thoughtful Learning and Authentic Assessment," considers the possibility of creating a social studies curriculum that promotes challenging, in-depth study on a limited number of essential topics. It raises three questions: The first is a rephrasing of the most important question curriculum planners can ask, What knowledge is of most worth? Here, it is asked in a more immediate way—Which social studies learnings are essential? Second, can assessment of student achievement on these essentials be made less bureaucratic and tedious and more authentic and satisfying? Here the concern is holding students accountable for their schoolwork while providing high standards to guide it. Third, what is the best way to use class time to support student learning?

This book is written for all people interested in improving history, geography, and civics education in the schools, but especially for the educators and parents in the thick of it: social studies curriculum planning groups. The planning committees that I have been fortunate to work with across the nation, especially in my three homes—Washington, Colorado, and Texas—have inspired and provoked much of the thinking that I share in these pages. I am grateful for the stimulating conversations we have had, most of them after school with stomachs growling and minds rattling, and I look forward to many more. Practical work, where something worthwhile is at stake, is its own reward.

1
Challenging Lessons on Essential Learnings

Somebody tell me about this Freedom train!

—*Langston Hughes*

THE GOAL OF THE SOCIAL STUDIES EDUCATOR IS TO HELP STUDENTS DEVELOP a deep, rich network of understandings related to a limited number of essential topics. Which topics are essential? Answering this question is the renewal committee's most important work.

Five Essential Learnings

Figure 1.1 (on page 2) represents my own nominations for the five most essential learnings of the K-12 social studies curriculum: the democratic ideal, cultural diversity, economic development, global perspective, and participatory citizenship.

Democratic Ideal

What is the democratic ideal? How, when, why, and where has it arisen in the course of human history? Compared to tyrannies, have democracies been long lasting or brief? Why? What constraints does the democratic ideal place on the majority? Are they fair? Are more constraints needed? What forms has democracy taken in the United States since its founding, and because of whose efforts? Was the

1

American Revolution fought for independence or democracy? What work is still needed to close the gap in the United States between the democratic ideal and daily practice? What circumstances—economic, political, social, international—undermine democracy? Could the Holocaust have happened in a democracy?

Figure 1.1 Five Essential Learnings Spiral Upward Through Each Grade

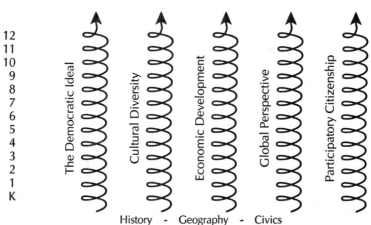

Cultural Diversity

Why is the United States a "nation of immigrants"? What does this mean? Are there any nations that are not? What challenges does cultural diversity pose to a society that is trying to express the democratic ideal? Can a society be multicultural and democratic at the same time? Must all peoples in a multicultural society subscribe to a common set of democratic values? How have societies typically responded to increased diversity? What does our past tell us are the conditions that support cooperation and toleration among ethnic groups? What happens when those conditions change? What has been the ethnic composition of North America since the first group of people crossed the land bridge? What composition is forecast for the future? How have majority ethnic groups treated ethnic minorities in each era of U.S. history? Was the Civil Rights movement of the 1960s the first such movement in U.S. history? Have there been similar movements in other nations? What is the extent of racism today? Can racism occur without scapegoating? prejudice? stereotyping? ethnocentrism?

Economic Development

How have societies organized themselves economically? What conditions have caused changes in the ways societies are organized? Has history taught us that there must be poor people in order for there to be rich people? Is the standard of living in the United States increasing or decreasing? How about in Japan, Mexico, Kenya, and Germany? What are your criteria? In what ways have nations become interdependent, and who benefits by it? How did the Third World become underdeveloped? Is there a way out? Do multinational corporations comprise a sort of world government? a world economic system? How has capitalism changed in the United States? How are capitalism, socialism, and communism similar and different? Does capitalism require democracy? Does democracy require capitalism? Did the Industrial Revolution change the way of life in North America for better or worse? How about in Japan? Is that revolution over? If so, what's next?

Global Perspective

What *is* a global perspective? How are the daily practices and ideas of the world's cultures different? Are the differences more important than the similarities? Are people everywhere basically the same? Are some cultural practices better than others? What civilizations have existed before ours and how have they shaped ours? What sorts of societies were there before nations? What conditions supported the development of nations? Does history teach us that there always will be nations? How have human societies changed the natural environment? What scenarios are forecast for human life on earth?

Participatory Citizenship

Why are people who live in societies organized under the democratic ideal expected to participate in civic life? What forms has this participation taken? What forms need to be promoted? What conditions have inhibited citizen participation in the past? What especially is the role of deliberation? Can individualism get out of hand? Has it? What does it mean to be *civic minded*? Does *everyone* in a democracy need to participate? How much decision making can be done by representatives without undermining the democratic ideal? What common moral codes must exist to sustain participatory citizenship?

Naturally enough, our students want to know why we are asking them to engage such questions, and they want to know why we consider in-depth work in history, geography, and civics to be an important and reliable path. That they don't at first understand why should not discourage us. There is nothing particularly self-evident to a child about the importance of these ideas. That they fail to see their importance simply underscores the need for students to explore them. Still, their principals, parents, and, especially, their teachers must themselves understand. They must themselves have grappled with questions of this sort and generated explanations for their importance. And they must share their explanations with their students. Let me share briefly my own.

First, such questions invite students to set off on historic adventures, the terrain and outcomes of which cannot be known in advance. These questions invite not just any adventures, but those that push us beyond our own experiences into the public world, into *civility* in all its forms. It is from that larger, shared vantage point that one is invited, in Michael Oakeshott's (1989) words, "to disentangle oneself, for a time, from the urgencies of the here and now and to listen to the conversation in which human beings forever seek to understand themselves." The ancient Greek plea, "Know Thyself," was not an exhortation to buy a self-help book, but to take up the great questions of humankind that have linked people together since the beginning of time. To avoid these questions is to be sentenced to a world crowded merely with happenings, devoid of perspective, of shared meaning, and, paradoxically, of individuality. It is an exile of the worst sort—Oakeshott calls it "a ceaseless flow of seductive trivialities"—involving neither reflection nor choice. The image that comes to my mind is a young person tied puppet-like to a Madison Avenue mogul.

Of course, there are disagreements as to what these big questions are. But such disagreement is not a problem, it is the very sort of debate that is needed. It is the most important conversation curriculum planners will have.

A second reason for engaging such questions is contained in a single word: judgment. The human adventure, the spectacle of being alive together, inheriting and creating a world for ourselves and our children, has no pat formulas. Consequently, judgment is crucial. Without it, knowledge is inert or, worse, dangerous. History teaches us that where judgment is absent, tyrants and dogma rush in. Consider the Nazi physicians who mastered the knowledge necessary to perform experimental surgery on prisoners but lacked the judgment that would have prevented them from undertaking that now infamous cruelty. Ponder the Nazi bureaucrat who blindly attended to his or her own affairs. Consider the European colonists in America who, without apparent hesitation, kidnapped then bought and sold Africans.

Without judgment, the work of democracy cannot be done. Imagine the following activities without benefit of judgment:

• the daily grind of public policy deliberation

• balancing the opposing tugs of public service and privacy in our own lives

• scrutinizing candidates at election time and supervising representatives once they have been elected (Parker 1988).

One historian has been clear about the role of judgment. Paul Gagnon notes that we demand judgment of all professionals, whether doctors, lawyers, teachers, chefs, accountants,or people in sales. And,

> we need it most in the profession of citizen, which, like it or not, we all are born into . . . . Judgment implies nothing less than wisdom . . . about human nature and society. It takes a sense of the tragic and of the comic to make a citizen of good judgment. It takes a bone-deep understanding of how hard it is to preserve civilization or to better human life, and of how these have nonetheless been done repeatedly in the past. It takes a sense of paradox, so as not to be surprised when failure teaches us more than victory does or when we slip from triumph to folly. And maybe most of all it takes a practiced eye for the beauty of work well done, in daily human acts of nurture (Gagnon 1988).

This book takes these questions seriously and considers how the social studies curriculum might be renewed in ways that help students take them seriously, too. Of course, they are challenging questions. But schools *can* be hotbeds of intellectual challenge, and they should be so for *all* our children. The fact that many young people will not go on to college after high school is no reason to exempt them from intellectual challenge. A school needs to challenge students intellectually not because they are or are not college bound, but because the mission of the school is learning.

It is *learning* that requires intellectual challenge. This is especially true of the kind of learning that is available when needed, the kind of learning that is useful—in civic affairs, on-the-job performance, and the rest of everyday life. In all of these, understandings (including misunderstandings) that already have been learned are brought to bear. Understandings that were developed under challenging circumstances are likely to be richer, deeper, and to have been cross-examined. Hence, they are more likely to be helpful (Resnick and Klopfer 1989).

I will elaborate later the elements of challenging circumstances, but, for now, I mean circumstances where (a) topics are studied in depth and (b) gathering and recalling facts are necessary *but not sufficient* for grappling with the problem or task at hand. These are circumstances in which the learner is required by the unit plan to gather and remember information *and* to go even further by analyzing, interpreting, and manipulating it.

But I am jumping ahead. Suffice it to say at this point that critically important understandings are at the heart of the social studies curriculum. To renew the social studies curriculum is to deliberate with others about which understandings are most important and then to create, systematically and artfully, a 13-year-long opportunity for students to build, refine, and apply those understandings.

Pervading Commitments

Three commitments pervade this book: First, the social studies curriculum can and must be genuinely thought-provoking for virtually all students. Second, the social studies curriculum should concentrate the intellectual resources of the student and the instructional resources of the school on a limited number of essential learnings that are treated in depth. The third commitment running through the book is democratic education. By this I generally mean education about democratic ideals and practices. More specifically, I mean the education of what interchangeably can be called "democratic" and "deliberative" character. At the heart of democratic character is the wherewithal to deliberate, which we will define as "careful consideration with a view to decision" (Gutmann 1987). Deliberation is democracy's primary virtue. "Is there no virtue

6

among us?" asked James Madison. "If there be not, no form of government can render us secure" (quoted in Draper 1982).

To educate children for democratic character is thus to educate them to share in ruling, in deliberation; to educate them to rule without discrimination or repression; to rule in such a way that daily life is moved closer to the democratic ideal, especially for those disadvantaged by present arrangements; and to accomplish this movement in an orderly enough way that democracy itself is not sacrificed to it. Whether we look to the Athens that executed Socrates, the Germany that embraced Hitler, the students in Tiananmen Square, the long era of Jim Crow in the United States, or the efforts of citizens in Eastern Europe and the Soviet Union to create democracies when they have been trained only to despotism, we can only conclude that democracy is not easy work. Lincoln fretted so about the public having the wherewithal to *do* this work that, like Jefferson before him and Martin Luther King, Jr. later, he put his faith in education:

> Let reverence for the laws be breathed by every American mother, to the lisping babe that prattles on her lap; let it be taught in schools, in seminaries, and in colleges; let it be written in Primers, spelling books, and in Almanacs; let it be preached from the pulpit, proclaimed in legislative halls, and enforced in halls of justice. And, in short, let it become the *political religion* of the nation.[1]

What we are after with this concern for democratic education is not a pious defense of the *status quo* or, worse, a sentimental longing for a Golden Age that never was. Both impulses are understandable when we consider the achievements of democracy to date, yet both stubbornly deny the work still to be done. Had the pioneers of our democracy been smug about what had been achieved so far—fighting off a despotic monarch and framing the Constitution and Bill of Rights—and ceased dreaming the democratic dream, voting would have remained the sole right of white male property owners; slaves would still be bought and sold; and non-Anglo immigrants would still be forced to shed their ethnic identities. Here is the point: Our forefathers and mothers did not rest on their laurels. They forged a yet more democratic future. And what we want are children who consider themselves heirs to this tradition—in Richard Rorty's

---

[1]From a speech by Abraham Lincoln to the Young Men's Lyceum of Springfield, January 27, 1838. Quoted in Freedman 1987.

(1989) words, "heirs to a tradition of increasing liberty and rising hope." We want children to come to think of themselves

> as proud and loyal citizens of a country that, slowly and painfully, threw off a foreign yoke, freed its slaves, enfranchised its women, restrained its robber barons and licensed its trade unions, liberalized its religious practices and broadened its religious and moral tolerance, and built colleges in which 50 percent of its population could enroll—a country that numbered Ralph Waldo Emerson, Eugene V. Debs, Susan B. Anthony, and James Baldwin among its citizens (Rorty 1989).

These then are the book's primary value judgments: The social studies curriculum renewal committee should create a thought-provoking social studies curriculum, concentrate instructional time on essential learnings, and do all this within an overarching and palpable commitment to democratic education. Three critical elements are brought to bear and are the focus of Chapter 6:

1. In-depth study: the sustained examination of a limited number of important topics. Superficial exposure to a vast array of topics undermines the habits of thoughtfulness we need to cultivate in social studies education.

2. Higher-order challenge: the design of curriculum and instruction that requires students to gather and use information in nonroutine applications. Future civic crises will be crises in part because of their novelty if we have nothing in our repertoire of experiences that tells us in quite enough detail what to do.

3. Authentic assessment: pointing students' schoolwork toward standard-setting exhibitions of learning. The social studies field traditionally has snubbed assessment, failing to use it to improve learning and instruction.

References

Draper, T. (1982). "Hume and Madison: The Secrets of Federalist Paper No. 10." *Encounter* 52: 47.

Freedman, R. (1987). *Lincoln*. New York: Clarion.

Gagnon, P. (November 1988). "Why Study History?" *The Atlantic Monthly* 262, 5: 43-44.

Gutmann, A. (1987). *Democratic Education*. Princeton, N.J.: Princeton University Press.

Oakeshott, M.M. (1989). "A Place of Learning." In *The Voice of Liberal Learning*, edited by T. Fuller. New Haven and London: Yale University Press.

Parker, W.C. (September/October 1988). "Why Ethics in Citizenship Education?" *Social Studies and the Young Learner* 1, 1: 4.

Resnick, L.B., and L.E. Klopfer, eds. (1989). *Toward the Thinking Curriculum: Current Cognitive Research*. Alexandria, Va.: Association for Supervision and Curriculum Development.

Rorty, R. (July 1989). "The Opening of American Minds." *Harpers Magazine* 279, 1670: 22.

2
Contexts of Renewal

In practice, the development of deliberative character is essential to
realizing the ideal of a democratically sovereign society . . . . The
willingness and ability to deliberate set morally serious people apart from
both sophists, who use clever argument to elevate their own interests into
self-righteous causes, and traditionalists, who invoke established
authority to subordinate their own reason to unjust causes . . . . Citizens
therefore have good reason to wonder how deliberative or democratic
character can be developed in children, and who can develop it.

—*Amy Gutmann*

THIS IS AN EXTRAORDINARY ERA. MATERIAL ABUNDANCE BUFFERS THE
average North American from a nearly incomprehensible litany of
social and environmental crises. The abundance nevertheless does
not satisfy. The crises go largely untended. The image is of an ostrich
burying its head not in the sand, but in its nest.

We probably are too close to all this to see it for what it is. Keen
observers returning to the United States after years abroad sometimes
have a clearer view. Stanley Meisler, for example, came home in 1989
after 21 years as a foreign correspondent. He was stunned by the
numbing excess of the U.S. supermarket shelf: Eleven brands of dog
food, row after row of convenience foods, and a cornucopia of salad
dressings: ranch, lite ranch, chunky ranch, spicy ranch, cajun ranch,
old fashioned ranch, ranch with garlic, and so on. Piling excess upon
excess, these supermarkets are housed in surrealistically huge and
ugly shopping malls that rise like pillboxes on guard against
simplicity, eccentricity, and both the real and imagined dangers of
city life (Meisler 1989).

Against this backdrop of runaway consumption loom the dispiriting problems of contemporary U.S. society. The crime and drug epidemics are presently without solution or coherent strategy, only stopgaps like increased arrests and longer prison sentences. The election of national leaders has been turned over to Madison Avenue image makers who market the candidates much like the salad dressings. The gap between rich and poor widens, hitting people of color the hardest, especially those who are women and children. The number of children in poverty is now four times greater than the number of elderly poor; and among poor blacks living in high-poverty tracts in the central cities, single-parent families outnumber married-couple families by three to one. All of these are affronts to participatory democracy and the development of deliberative character.

Meanwhile, the ozone weakens and rain forests are cleared. Garbage mounts north of the equator as starvation spreads south of it. Celebrities are mistaken for heroes, money for meaning, cul-de-sac for community. It is as if Chief Seattle's sad reverie of 1854 is coming true:

> The whites, too, shall pass—perhaps sooner than the other tribes .... When the buffalo are all slaughtered, the wild horses all tamed, the secret corners of the forest heavy with the scent of many men, and the view of the ripe hills blotted by the talking wires, where is the thicket? Gone. Where is the eagle? Gone. And what is it to say goodbye to the swift and the hunt, to the end of living and the beginning of survival? We might understand if we knew what it was that the White Man dreams, what he describes to his children on the long winter nights, what visions he burns into their minds, so they will wish for tomorrow. But we are savages. The White Man's dreams are hidden from us (from Brewster 1989).

Some scientists wonder aloud whether humanity is *able* to solve its problems (Ornstein and Erlich 1989). They argue that the human nervous system has not evolved to a point where comprehension of the long term is possible. According to this biological explanation, human attention is quickly seduced by short-term crises while apparently less immediate, and thus less newsy, but ultimately more threatening trends, are ignored. Hostage takings, airplane crashes, terrorist hijackings, and gruesome local crimes readily capture the headlines; the destruction of rain forests, the rich/poor gap, and demographic trends are strangely absent in the evening news.

By sociological and political accounts, the public has become too private-minded to cope with common problems (see Bellah et al.

1985 and Barber 1984). "The Public seems to be lost," Dewey (1925) observed decades ago. "It is certainly bewildered." It has lost its sense of balance. Especially in North America it has become too dependent on creature comforts—on *shopping*—to curtail its consumption, and too devoted to "singing my own song" and "doing it my way" to care much about community life. All this might be summed up in an idea—an "ism"—that is relatively new: individualism. As the keen French observer, de Toqueville, noted in the 1840s, this is a modern invention:

> 'Individualism' is a word recently coined to express a new idea. Our fathers only knew about egoism. Egoism is a passionate and exaggerated love of self which leads a man to think of all things in terms of himself and to prefer himself to all. Individualism is a calm and considered feeling which disposes each citizen to isolate himself from the mass of his fellows and withdraw into the circle of family and friends; with this little society formed to his taste, he gladly leaves the greater society to look after itself (de Toqueville 1969).

Whichever explanation one finds stronger, it is quite clear that in the midst of all this, an increasingly uneasy public has put its hopes in, of all places, the schools. It is as though teachers and their students might solve problems that the public is reluctant even to face.

Amid these unrealistic expectations, let's attempt to be realistic about what is and isn't feasible within the scope of the school's social studies curriculum. Let's try to walk the same path that a social studies curriculum planning committee must walk: a middle path between dogma and chaos. This is a moderate path among the extremes of social amnesia, social zealotry, and cynicism. The first of these ignores all the ways social realities intrude upon school practices, for example, how tracking helps to sort children into occupational hierarchies. Zealotry pretends the school can rescue society. Cynicism gives up grappling with these matters, preferring simply to moan.[1]

In fact, the problems are workable. Granted, schools are modest among social institutions. They are not suspended above the fray but are woven into it. Consequently, they haven't the autonomy to change society (let alone rescue it), and they cannot single-handedly solve the public's problems. Yet schools do have a measure of

---

[1]Leaning in the direction of social amnesia are the recent education critiques of Diane Ravitch and E.D. Hirsch; erring in the direction of social zealotry are the critiques of John Dewey, at least in so far as he assumed schools were autonomous sites of social *transformation*.

influence on the civic health of society. This influence is determined in no small measure by the commitments and intentions of the adults who work in them. If school personnel are awake to the possibilities of a truly public education, one that seeks a democratic commonwealth and nurtures overarching ideals and cultural pluralism, then they can accomplish a good deal. They can, to take just one modest example, teach history. They can assure its central place in the curriculum every day in every grade, even in the primary grades where it is all too easily lost to a contentless "skills" curriculum. They can make sure that every history lesson has its geography, its relationship to other lessons, and its dilemmas for young citizens to weigh—a history alive with the multiple voices of our past, not just the European settlers, presidents, and wars. They can prod students to explore their own cultural identities, their own sense of fairness, their own conception of the greater good. The result can be students who have at least some of the knowledge, habits, and moral vision needed to deliberate inventively and democratically on the public's problems.

Lacking these commitments and intentions, teachers and administrators may find themselves participating only in the preparation of the self-centered individualists de Toqueville described. Clearly, this is a breach of public education. It ignores the imperatives that undergird education in a society that is endeavoring to express the democratic ideal. These imperatives are uniquely democratic (you wouldn't find them, say, in Libya or China). Chief among them are preparing the public to deliberate common problems together, without discrimination or repression, and making persons in power behave intelligently and honestly. This is popular sovereignty—government of, by, and for the people. Preparing for popular sovereignty, to hold well the "office of citizen," is why we have public schools.

The measure of influence, then, that schools can wield on the civic health of society exists in the preparation they provide for the social demands of democracy. This influence is not exerted through impossible abstractions like "citizenship education," but through the actual, local ways schools are organized, the relationships they build with the community, the situations in which they place children, the conditions of learning they are able to provide, the adult models they present, and the particular understandings they exhort their students to construct.

Typically, a social studies curriculum committee deals only with the last of these: subject matter. This is understandable, but unfortunate nonetheless. After all, the curriculum is bound up with the ways a school is organized and the ways a community treats its educational responsibilities. Both the school organization and, beyond this, the community, shape and constrain the curriculum, sometimes reinforcing and extending it, sometimes undermining it.

The Influence of School Organization on Curriculum

Those who seek to renew the social studies curriculum must understand that the way the school is organized is relevant to their work. In a fundamental way, school organization *determines* the subject matters to which children are exposed as well as the quality of opportunities they are provided for learning it. Because school organization constitutes an influence of the first order; we need to try to understand it. Let's consider a number of examples: departmentalization, testing, tracking, personnel decisions, and the heart of the school: its mission.

Departmentalization

The organization of secondary schools into subject-area departments has effectively prohibited implementation of an idea that just about everybody seems to agree is a good one (and one that is neither expensive nor complicated): integrating the study of American history, literature, and art. The perspectives afforded history when it is entered imaginatively through fiction, when it is made real in primary documents and in biographies of key players, and when it is revealed through the aesthetic sensibilities of the historical period in question all compel a rich and lively examination of people, events, and forces.

Observers who haven't worked in schools might be unable to fathom why such a simple and obvious improvement over standard practice is not by now standard practice. The answer is quite easy, at least for those of us who have worked in schools: The organization of a school building and its faculty into subject divisions creates a physical arrangement *and a building culture* that makes this idea nearly unworkable. Of course, there are instances when an English teacher and a social studies teacher work as a team to provide an interdisciplinary "American Studies" course, and one hears now and then of the history teacher who supplements the text with historical

14

fiction. But these are exceptions, not the rule, precisely because the fragmentation of the school into departmental subcultures makes them difficult.

Testing

It is possible for a school's testing practices to drive the curriculum and the learning climate of the school in undesirable directions. Legislators and administrators have so exaggerated the importance of scores on standardized tests of basic skills that subject matter not emphasized on these tests is shoved aside. This includes even crucial content such as ethnic diversity and the meaning of democracy.

Even when social studies is built firmly into the *written* curriculum, the testing frenzy can effectively exclude it from the *taught* curriculum. One has only to listen to teachers: "We do math and reading in the morning when the kids are fresh. We do . . . social studies in the afternoon, if there is a chance." Or, "I'm not going to do any more social studies until after Christmas" (Smith 1978).

Testing the three Rs has so thoroughly sapped the assessment energies of schools that there has been virtually no creative thinking about assessment in social studies. Students are given diplomas in return for nothing more than a transcript indicating accrued seat time (having "taken" a requisite number of social studies credits and not failed). This indicates practically nothing about the abilities and understandings that graduates have or have not achieved, or about the standards used to assess them.

Tracking

Tracking, too, has a powerful curricular effect (Oakes 1985). What may begin simply as ability grouping becomes tracking once it becomes clear that students remain in the same ability groups. In the early grades, students might be divided into three groups for instructional purposes. Group A gets the highest quality curriculum. These students stand a better chance of being engaged in more thought-provoking study with less drill, more challenge, better resources, more primary documents, more discussion and critical thinking, guest speakers, art and literature, and so on. Meanwhile, Group C receives the lowest quality curriculum with less challenge, less discussion, and more drill. Group B gets something in between. By the 12th grade, we notice that the so-called ability groups are still intact! Now, Group A is taking advanced placement courses, Group C is taking auto mechanics or clerical training, and students in Group B—the so-called "mid kids"—are meandering through a rarely challenging "regular" curriculum.

It is quite possible that remediation is not the function of these grouping practices, though often this is the rationale. Rather, schools track students in order to perform in straightforward fashion their allocating function in society. That function is to allocate status and occupations, that is, to sort students into a career ladder where, as in the corporate world, there is little room at the top and lots at the middle and bottom. Since in a society dedicated to equal opportunity no one would stand for schools doing this randomly, the practice of ability grouping is put into place. As a consequence, the sorting practice looks both natural, neutral, and meritocratic. Students have only their own failures to blame—low ability, laziness, lack of perseverance or intelligence, and so on. This has been compared to a con game in which the victims come eventually to blame themselves for being so gullible (see Parker 1985).

Another organizational reason why schools track students is that tracked students can be more easily managed. By reducing the variation of student knowledge, ability, and learning style in a classroom, we have reduced its complexity. The heterogeneous demands of teaching have been made more homogeneous: Because students are less diverse, instruction can be less diverse, and weak instructional strategies like "telling" can be employed at length without causing the behavior management problems that surely would follow in a heterogeneous classroom (McNeil 1986).

The point I want to make here, however, is that tracking results in *curriculum differentiation*. It is not that the various tracks are getting different versions of the same thing; rather, they are getting something different altogether. I am surprised at my noneducator friends who assume that the school curriculum is basically the same for all students. At the surface, it *is*—all students have "history," "English," and "mathematics." Most students study "government." But there are compelling data that show that low- and high-track students study different topics and are encouraged to think and develop themselves in different ways. In mind as I write this are nearby high schools where upper-track students take American history as part of an integrated "Humanities Block." Students in the lower tracks are not so lucky.

High-track students are more likely to be challenged to study high-status topics emphasized on college entrance exams, to engage in higher-order thinking, and to develop attitudes of self-reliance. Low-track students are less likely to be challenged in this way. Instead, they are more likely to memorize lists and study topics with immediate vocational value. This suggests that schools may pose as pure meritocracies where only student ability determines student success; however, through the organizational practice of tracking, they become a blend of meritocracy and aristocracy—not just *responding* to student differences but, by exposing different students to different content and opportunities, *producing* student differences (Oakes 1985).

Personnel Selection

Personnel selection practices can undermine a curriculum committee's best work. Let's look at one aspect of personnel selection, teacher knowledge. Clearly, teachers need to know a great deal in order to perform their craft well. We might simplify recent research on this matter by pointing to two domains of a teacher's knowledge base: what they know about methods of teaching, and what they know about the subject they are teaching. But the knowledge base is even more complex than this, for the methods of teaching interact with the subject matters (see Stodolsky 1988).

Teaching methods that help students develop understandings of, for instance, popular sovereignty and the relationship between stereotyping and prejudice are different from those that help students acquire information (e.g., the number of amendments in the Bill of Rights) or that help students practice a skill (e.g., accessing a database at a desktop computer). Thus, the methods of "direct instruction" popularized by Madeline Hunter may well be less widely applicable than was thought. In particular, they may be more appropriate to the teaching of skills than the development of understandings (Rosenshine 1986). The implications for the social studies curriculum are important because understandings outnumber skills in social studies. What caused the revolutions in France, Russia, and China? Can revolutions be predicted? Why is the southern hemisphere poorer than the northern hemisphere? Are all societies ethnically diverse? Is prejudice universal? What conditions permitted the rise of the Nazis? These aren't "skills."

We can see, then, that the teacher who knows an array of methods *and* who knows which methods come alive with different kinds of content has a clear advantage. Likewise, the teacher who knows a topic deeply will probably be better able to distinguish among and catalogue relevant ideas, information, and skills. Let's compare two teachers.

Mrs. Trujillo and Mr. Langland were hired to teach American history to 8th grade students. Mrs. Trujillo has a degree in U.S. history and knows a good deal about the founding of the United States. Mr. Langland's degree is in English. He has a cursory familiarity with the founding. Their units on the topic are dramatically different. Mr. Langland's students read about the Revolution in their social studies textbook, listen to his explanation, fill out worksheets based on what they read about, and map the major battles. The unit lasts five days.

Mrs. Trujillo's unit is spread out over a month. She continually seeks out historical fiction related to the War for Independence and the events that preceded it, and presently her students read the Colliers' *War Comes to Willy Freeman* and Fast's *April Morning*. She knows that *Willy* is easier reading for her 8th graders than *Morning*, but she knows that both, with her help, deliver her students imaginatively into what must have been the most excruciating dilemma faced by the new Americans—independence or loyalty? Mrs. Trujillo chooses *Willy* over *My Brother Sam is Dead*, also by the Colliers, because she believes the book "multiculturalizes" her unit and renders it morally challenging to her students by developing an additional theme: the experiences of African Americans and women, for whom the British and the Americans were not so different after all. She has them write on the question, "What was the American Dream for each of the young people we came to know in these books?"

Having opened with literature, she follows with primary documents. These include Thomas Paine's argument for revolution and Charles Inglis' argument against it. Mrs. Trujillo teaches her students how to search for additional documents in the school library to judge their relevance to this particular dilemma. But what motivates their search? Using a cooperative learning method called "structured academic controversy," she assigns them to teams of four to debate both sides of the issue. The essay question on the exam asks the students to evaluate the strength of the arguments for and against revolution.

This sketch underscores one point: School administrators can go a long way toward increasing student achievement of the planned curriculum by ensuring that teachers know deeply the topics they are supposed to teach and can use an array of methods to help students learn.

Mission

The school's mission is the understood reason for the school's existence. The mission is larger than the curriculum and more than the opportunities provided students to learn it. The mission incorporates these as well as the quality of relationships between students and their principals, classmates, and teachers; the roles they are expected to play; and the school's reward system, ceremonies, and personnel policies. Together, these aspects of the daily world of the school are the school's mission. They announce whether learning, or something else, is the school's purpose. If the mission is unambiguously pointed toward challenging and helping students to learn the planned curriculum, if the organization actually revolves around student learning, *if this is why the school exists*, then the sheer presence of the school encourages learning.

But observation indicates that learning is not necessarily the mission of all schools. Other purposes compete, and prominent among them is the celebration of athletic challenge. From the morning announcements detailing team wins and losses, practice schedules, and upcoming pep assemblies, to the notorious tradition of favoring faculty applicants who can coach sports teams, academic learning is threatened by athletic competition. I have been struck in my work with curriculum planning committees by the large number of teachers who agree that team sports have eaten away at the fabric of the school. Everyone's favorite example is the administrator who excuses coaches early from faculty meetings and curriculum renewal programs so they can tend to their teams and games. The organization thus announces its priorities in no uncertain terms. When I am working with faculties in the afternoon on curriculum development issues, and this is even in top-rated school districts, I have come to expect an exodus of the coaches to the playing fields midway through the program.

Another ulterior mission of schools is the propagation of teen culture. Open displays of vigorous intellectual effort in middle and high schools often are discouraged by the dominant peer culture (and often by adults as well). Too often, schools are given over to mixing, courting, clothing displays, and getting ready for the after-school job.

The Community: A Resource and Ally

The local community should be brought directly into the service of the social studies curriculum. The community has a "curriculum" of its own, which can reinforce and enrich the school's curriculum, or contradict and undermine it. The attitudes, values, and knowledge the community brings to children through its media, shopping malls, street corners, workplaces, minority-majority relations, entertainment, rituals, norms of social decency, manner of deliberating public problems, inclusion of people of color, and its expectations of the schools—all of this *instructs* (Postman 1986). If the community's lessons run counter to the school's lessons, then school learning can be isolated, devalued, and trivialized.

But imagine what might happen if the community's curriculum were actually to support the school's. Think what the results might be if social studies learning were promoted and rewarded by community organizations; if high school students were expected to deliberate proposed public policies; if employers were to require teenage job applicants to exhibit their understandings of the world map, ethnic diversity, and democratic practices; if parents were to demand that athletics take a back seat to learning!

Of course, there is no monolithic "community." The school is located, to some extent, in a multicultural community, so there are a number of communities with which, and in which, it must operate. These are communities of social class, religion, ethnicity, and color. But there is a common political ideal: democracy. When the school recognizes both of these things, and to its bones practices them in its rituals, awards and rewards, climate, discipline policy, and curriculum, it serves as a working example of a multicultural community organized under the democratic ideal.

Recommendations

The curriculum renewal committee may prefer to tread lightly on organizational matters, leaving them to administrators, and devote itself to the enormously challenging task of selecting the content and experiences that comprise the curriculum. And it is hardly realistic to expect a curriculum committee, already faced with the awesome task of mobilizing students, curriculum materials, and faculty, to mobilize the community as well. Nevertheless, I want to encourage some measure of attention, whatever can be mustered, to school organization and community relations. Curriculum deliberation is more encompassing than we might at first surmise. Ultimately, a curriculum plan should precede organizational flow charts and building floor plans, not tag along behind them. Here are a few recommendations.

School Organization

The social studies curriculum committee should recommend that administrators initiate a series of faculty discussions on the school's mission. The committee members might propose that learning the planned curriculum be the mission. Naturally, such discussions should include assessments of other candidates for the school's mission: athletic competition, teen socializing, job training, day care, college preparation, and the like. It should be helpful when contemplating a public school's mission to recall the debates surrounding their founding. I have been struck by the arguments used by civic leaders who wanted to convince their neighbors that public schools were needed, even if expensive. Did they argue that public schools were needed to train young athletes? To inculcate religious precepts? To prepare children for the labor force? To help them get into college? To provide a common place where youth could meet and court one another? No. None of these. The argument that won over the public was a *civic* argument. It was that all children need schooling because popular sovereignty depends on it.

Horace Mann, speaking in 1845 for public schooling, knew well that democracies are rare and usually short-lived. He knew, too, that "the people," as in "government of, by, and for the people," were a nation of immigrants, many of whom were bred under dictators of one stripe or another. The situation was dangerous and the remedy was education:

> The great moral attribute of self-government (popular sovereignty) cannot be born and matured in a day; and if children are not trained to it, we only prepare ourselves for disappointment if we expect it from grown men . . . . As the fitting apprenticeship for despotism consists in being trained to despotism, so the fitting apprenticeship for self-government consists in being trained to self-government (Mann 1845/1946).

Community

School representatives should meet with local employers, both public and private, to talk about ways employers might hold job applicants accountable for school learning. In particular, I envision employers agreeing to require of a job applicant, in addition to the firm's job application form, indications of the applicant's ability to write, read, and compute, as well as participate as a citizen in a democratic community. Applicants might be asked to submit a portfolio that includes a school transcript, a written analysis of a public policy controversy the community faces and, as an indicator of computational ability, an explanation of statistics on a recent local election or demographic trends in the neighborhoods. Selection of the items to be included in the portfolio (as we see in Chapter 6) should be an important part of the curriculum committee's work.

Second, the committee might assemble an Essential Learnings in Social Studies Advisory Board to evaluate the current K-12 social studies program, looking especially for important subject matter strands. This work would involve poring through written curriculum documents as well as interviewing teachers, department heads, principals, and coordinators. The board might concentrate its inquiry on particular strands, such as democracy, global perspective, and cultural diversity, or it could be asked simply to "dive in and report back." Its work is done when it presents to the curriculum committee a portrait of the existing social studies curriculum and a critique.

The board would be composed of local professors of history, government, and geography, as well as people working in related occupations (cartographers, social workers, judges, politicians, librarians, journalists).[2]

It is crucial that women and people of color are well-represented on the board, not only because democracy and cultural diversity are major historical themes in the social studies curriculum, but because the school must operate in a multicultural milieux. An advisory board of white Christian males might be rigorous in its attention to that fact, but a multicultural board is more likely to place a multicultural point of view in the curriculum.

Third, the committee might specify in the written curriculum a process for parent involvement in social studies schoolwork. One form this might take is identifying ways for teachers to involve parents, perhaps two weekends a month, in their child's social studies homework (see Brandt 1989) or requiring students to talk with a parent about some especially interesting and important part of schoolwork. Children who are building an understanding of

---

[2]In Howard County, Maryland, where this was done with the science curriculum, 62 scientists submitted applications to serve on the board (see Utterback and Kalin 1989).

democracy might, for example, talk with someone at home about a nation presently in the news that is struggling for democratic reform Children studying economic transformation might work with someone at home to trace family history back to the period before the industrial revolution when relatives may have lived and worked in extended families on a farm or plantation. Recent immigrants from agricultural societies can provide first-hand international comparisons.

Personnel Selection

Clearly, teachers and principals must be properly educated for their work toward the school's mission. Minimally, and considering only their college preparation, this means that elementary teachers should have an undergraduate major in an academic subject along with some coursework in the other teaching fields, or a distributed major that includes significant learning in each of the teaching fields. Secondary teachers of social studies should at least have an undergraduate major in the field of their primary teaching responsibility.

Principals should have this education and more: minimally, an undergraduate major in an academic field and a graduate degree in an academic field or in a field of education relevant to leading a school. This should help to rule out the principal whose knowledge base is peripheral to the school's mission (e.g., the principal who rises through the ranks of the building's athletic program).

The intent of these personnel selection recommendations is to support, if not ensure, the knowledge base of those who must carry out the school's mission. Another form of support is through the building's staff development program, which need not always be aimed at instructional improvement, since instruction cannot be assumed always to be the problem. It also can inform teachers' knowledge of the subject they are trying to help their students learn.

Tracking

We are struggling in the United States to fashion a society where cultural differences are celebrated and ethnocentrism and racism are neither tempting nor tolerated. And we are attempting to create schools where *all* students have access to powerful understandings and abilities and where *all* students are expected to explore and exhibit democratic character. This is clearly an ambitious aim. Just as clearly, a gap exists between this ideal and the present state of affairs. In keeping with the school's civic mission, the gap must be narrowed.

One promising and feasible alternative to tracking can be found in the collection of group learning procedures developed under the rubric "cooperative learning." In these strategies (e.g., "Jigsaw"), the organization of the classroom is fundamentally altered. Student-to-student interaction on the subject at hand is combined with altered accountability and reward systems. Students are grouped heterogeneously and made positively dependent upon one another for increasing their academic learning. Cooperative learning also develops cooperative skills, mutual concern among students of different ethnic groups and circumstances, and self-esteem. There is good evidence to suggest that cooperative learning in heterogeneous classrooms, when well structured, can achieve all of these goals better than individualistic learning in homogeneous classrooms (Slavin 1986). Hence, a mixed student population can hardly be viewed as a disadvantage.

Assessment

Schools need to rethink assessment. They can and should hold students accountable for grappling with the essential learnings of the social studies program. There are a number of ways to go about this—by using mass-produced standardized tests (e.g., I.T.B.S.), formal and informal measures designed by individual teachers, and tests provided by publishers to accompany their textbooks. All of these have a place in the assessment of students' academic progress, but another form is desperately needed: formal, authentic, benchmark assessments placed strategically in the K-12 social studies curriculum.

I recommend placing these at the end of the elementary, middle or junior high, and high school years. These assessments need to be challenging yet reasonable, and they need clearly to reflect the curriculum committee's best hopes for students. While I elaborate this recommendation in Chapter 6, let me note here that district committees with which I have worked recently have imagined benchmark assessments like these:

At the end of elementary school

• Writing/Civics/History: Students write a summary of a current public controversy drawn from school life and tell how a courageous and civic-minded American they have studied (e.g., Sojourner Truth, James Madison) might decide to act on the issue.

• Geography: Students sketch a physical map of North America from memory and locate (given coordinates) five cities.

At the end of middle/junior high school

• Writing/Civics/History: Students write an analysis of a current public controversy facing their community and draw a historical comparison.

• Geography: Students sketch a world landform map from memory with continents labeled and locate (given coordinates) 10 capital cities,

At the end of high school

• Writing/Geography/Civics: Students identify a current international conflict and write an analysis of it that draws historical parallels and represents the multiple perspectives involved. Students also reproduce from memory a political map (with salient landforms) of the region.

• Citizenship: Students answer correctly 90 percent of the questions on the citizenship test given to immigrants seeking naturalization.

* * *

Curriculum renewal is inevitably a social and political activity. It must respond creatively and sensibly to its mandate to prepare children to hold the office of citizen. If it can muster the necessary energy, the curriculum renewal committee will not only adopt textbooks and recommend a curriculum plan; it will recommend alterations in school organization and community support—changes that will increase the chances that students will learn the curriculum. This is taking curriculum renewal seriously.

References

Bellah, R.N., R. Madsen, W.M. Sullivan, A. Swidler, and S.M. Tipton (1985). *Habits of the Heart*. New York: Harper and Row.

Brandt, R. (October 1989). "On Parents and Schools: A Conversation with Joyce Epstein." *Educational Leadership* 47, 2: 24-27.

Brewster, D. (September 13, 1989). "The End of Living and the Beginning of Survival." *The Seattle Weekly*, page 2.

de Toqueville, A. (1969). *Democracy in America*. Translated by George Lawrence. Edited by J.P. Mayer. New York: Doubleday, Anchor Books.

Dewey, J. (1925). *The Public and its Problems*. Chicago: Swallow Press.

Mann, H. (1946). *Ninth Annual Report of the Secretary of the Board of Education*. Boston: Dutton & Wentworth.

McNeil, L.M. (1986). *Contradictions of Control*. New York: Routledge.

Meisler, S. (August 6, 1989). "Fear in the Land of Plenty." *The Seattle Times*, page 16.

Oakes, J. (1985). *Keeping Track: How Schools Structure Inequality*. New Haven, Conn.: Yale University Press.

Ornstein, R. and P. Erlich. (1989). *New World New Mind: Moving Toward Conscious Evolution*. New York: Doubleday.

Parker, W.C. (Summer 1985). "The Urban Curriculum and the Allocating Function of Schools." *The Educational Forum* 49, 4: 445-450.

Postman, N. (1986). *Amusing Ourselves to Death*. New York: Penguin.

Rosenshine, B. (1986). "Unsolved Issues in Teaching Content: A Critique of a Lesson on Federalist Paper No. 10." *Teaching and Teacher Education* 2, 4: 301-308.

Slavin, R.E. (1986). *Using Student Team Learning*, 3rd ed. Baltimore: Center for Research on Elementary and Middle Schools.

Smith, M.L. (1978). "Teaching and Science Education in Fall River." In *Case Studies in Science Education*, Vol. I, edited by R.E. Stake and J. Easley. Urbana-Champaign, Ill.: Center for Instructional Research and Curriculum Evaluation, University of Illinois.

Stodolsky, S.S. (1988). *The Subject Matters*. Chicago, Ill.: University of Chicago Press.

Utterback, P.H., and M. Kalin. (October 1989). "A Community-Based Model of Curriculum Evaluation." *Educational Leadership* 47, 2: 49-50.

3
Deliberation
for Change

It is not that, knowing the answer myself, I perplex other people. The truth is rather that I try to infect them with the perplexity I feel myself.

—*Socrates*

A Case Study

AT 3:45 P.M. ON A TUESDAY AFTERNOON IN OCTOBER, THE SOCIAL STUDIES curriculum renewal committee of the Vista City school district was called to order. The committee chair, June Rowentz, was the district's curriculum director. She had selected three teachers from the district elementary schools, three from the middle schools, and three from the high schools. The committee was to spend the school year studying and improving the district's social studies curriculum.

Committee members from whom we hear are Martha, a 10th grade world history teacher; Louise, an 11th grade "advanced placement" American history teacher; Bill, who teaches a 7th grade language arts/geography block; Ed, who teaches an 8th grade language arts/American history block; Marjorie, a 4th grade teacher; and Ellen, a 2nd grade teacher.

Last year, June had convened and chaired a curriculum planning committee for mathematics; next year, she will do the same in reading/language arts, followed in the next year by science and, in the next, music and the arts. This year was social studies' turn.

Session #1

After introductions, June put the first issue before the committee: parental involvement in curriculum planning. She proposed that three parents be invited to join the committee—one each from an elementary, middle, and high school. Martha, the 10th grade world history teacher, liked the idea. She thought including parents at the outset would communicate in no uncertain terms the committee's interest in their views and a commitment to working together. Bill added that the parent members might be encouraged to report on the committee's work at PTA meetings and, more ambitiously, help cultivate support for the schools among parents who were typically aloof.

Ellen, the 2nd grade teacher, was more ambitious still. "It would be great if the parent members could motivate all the apathetic parents who just turn education over to the schools. But it would be even better if they would get the fast-food restaurants to give a history and geography test before hiring any of our kids."

Marjorie, the 4th grade teacher, cautioned the group against the involvement of parents at this planning stage. "After all," she observed, "these are lay people. Curriculum planning requires both curriculum expertise and classroom teaching experience. We're going to have to use well the little time we have together, and I don't want to have to spend it teaching parents what has become second nature to those of us in the classroom. Plus, parents would get us off track by raising issues like sex education, evolution, secular humanism, and all the other red herrings."

The group agreed with Marjorie, and vowed to return to the issue later in the year when parental involvement might be more productive.

June then proposed that the group use a procedure, based loosely on the work of Ralph Tyler, that would involve four steps: identifying objectives, identifying learning experiences that would achieve those objectives, organizing those experiences across the grades, and planning an evaluation that would be conducted every two years.

"That sounds reasonable," said Bill. "But who are *we* to select objectives? That's why we have a school board. And what about the curriculum guidelines that were just published by the state education office? Can't we simply lift our objectives from those?"

"We could," June responded, "but the state guidelines are just that—guidelines, not objectives. And as far as our school board is concerned, we're the curriculum planning committee. Of course, what we plan here has to be approved by the board, but we are the body to whom the board has authorized the decision making."

Martha chimed in: "Wait a minute. I can't imagine that we have to reinvent the wheel here. I mean, it isn't as though we don't already have a social studies curriculum. We *do*. It has goals, objectives, and a scope-and-sequence plan, which, by the way, is posted on a wall in the administration building. And a lot of people think it's just fine. Actually, I presume we all know that most teachers ignore it. New teachers in my building aren't even shown a copy of it, and the better teachers brag that they don't use it. But, we do have one. Why don't we begin by evaluating it? If it's adequate, we can leave it as it is and work on getting everyone in each building to teach it. If it's flawed, we can fix it."

"*Start* with evaluation?" This seemed backward to Marjorie. Furthermore, she argued that starting with an examination of the existing curriculum would constrain the group, closing off what she called "curriculum dreaming." "Let's not limit ourselves to the status quo," she pleaded. "Let's not settle for something that's merely 'adequate.' Let's envision a curriculum for the 21st century, not the 20th, one that really—I mean *really*, not just rhetorically—educates for democratic citizenship in a multicultural society. We could actually do it you know. It is feasible."

But Louise, the 11th grade advanced placement (AP) American history teacher, thought Martha had the right idea. "There already exists a social studies curriculum, at least on paper. Let's evaluate it critically, noting the good and the bad. Few of us plan our lessons by first stating objectives, so why should we limit ourselves like that here?"

"Sounds good," Ed said. "But my evaluation of the existing curriculum is going to be better if I have some idea of the alternatives." Ed had taught 8th grade language arts and American history, as a block, for ten years. By his own admission, he would be hard pressed to imagine any other way to organize the course.

Marjorie liked Ed's idea. "If we're going to start by examining the curriculum we already have, we won't be able to do it critically unless we have alternatives in mind. We will only see what is there, not what is missing. So, I think we're going to have to skip back and forth between studying our curriculum and studying alternatives."

June nodded approvingly. If they were to begin with an evaluation of the existing curriculum, as Martha had proposed, then they would have to do their homework first. "If we're to evaluate well, it seems to me that we need to know what other school districts across the nation are doing and what the professional organizations are recommending. That way, we can put our curriculum in perspective. For example, the National Council for the Social Studies has three different K-12 curriculums. Also, there's an organization of historians that has published a curriculum that beefs up the teaching of history, even in the elementary grades, and California has done something different, too."

"It sure has," Louise added. "California evidently thinks 11th graders are going to remember what they learned in the 5th grade about colonization. That'll be the day."

June nodded her head. "Well, I think they provide some options for us to review. At any rate, this is my point: By learning about some alternatives and comparing them with what we have now, we can work our way to something better than what we have now."

"And better than the alternatives, maybe," added Louise.

"Well, if we're going to start with something other than objectives," Marjorie said, "it ought to be with our aim. You know, our vision of what kind of people we want Vista City graduates to be."

Ed: "Wouldn't it be simpler and more realistic if we looked at the new textbooks on the market? I mean, why should we dream up a curriculum for which there will be no materials?"

June: "But, Ed, I am not very comfortable with letting textbook publishers in New York and Boston and Chicago decide what we do here in Vista City."

Ed: "Well, I'm not so comfortable with that, either, June. But I'm even less comfortable at the prospect of us producing an eccentric curriculum and then having to produce all the resources that support it ourselves. I mean, we can't just *ignore* the resource issue."

"Ed's got a point," Bill added. "I have a friend in Valley Grove who had to find all her own world history material because her social studies committee put world history in the 7th grade curriculum. Publishers typically write world history materials for the 9th or 10th grades. So, she is left holding the curriculum guide without the resources she needs."

Ellen: "And in 2nd grade, their curriculum committee decided to teach about explorers and pioneers. When it came time to implement it, good material had yet to be located. So, you can guess what happened. The 2nd grade teachers did what they usually do."

June: "What's that?"

Ellen: "They taught reading and mathematics."

June: "*No* social studies?"

Ellen: "*No* social studies. Well, virtually no social studies. Just the holidays—you know, Independence Day and Thanksgiving. You can't really call that teaching social studies. It's funny to think about all the upset parents who are worried about today's students lacking knowledge of history and geography. I mean, it's really no mystery. Kids aren't learning history and geography because it isn't being taught!"

June: "I see your point, Ellen. We want to dream, but not hallucinate. We don't want to create a social studies plan for which there are no materials, or for which materials selection is so difficult that teachers will simply not teach social studies.

"But let's get back to the issue Marjorie raised a moment ago: our *aim*. What sort of workers do we want Vista City graduates to be?"

"Workers!?" Bill was perturbed. "Who said anything about workers, June? Marjorie said *people*. It sounds to me like you've been spending too much time with the Chamber of Commerce—you know, the guys who assume schools exist to train the labor force. That's hardly what history is for, or geography. We have to keep our eye on civic affairs, not the factory and the stock market. Since we can't teach everything, we have to choose. And I think we should choose to cultivate Thomas Jeffersons and Susan B. Anthonys, people whose first commitment is to public interests, not to themselves and their precious little wants."

Marjorie: "Well, what's wrong with turning out good workers? I thought all those blue-ribbon commissions were complaining that the U.S. is falling behind Japan and Germany."

Ed: "Falling behind in what way?"

Marjorie: "*Economically.* Our workers don't seem to know enough to get the job done. Their reading, writing, and mathematics skills are deficient."

Ellen: "And they evidently can't cooperate with one another or tackle intellectual problems together in teams."

Marjorie: "Right, cooperation skills, too. All of which adds up to our falling behind in productivity and standard of living and, soon, all the other countries where the schools take seriously their role in preparing the work force."

Bill: "Well, I think we need to get our heads out of our wallets long enough to remember the civic purpose of schools, especially in democracies. The reason we have free public education here is not to win the electronics race with Japan and Germany but to enable all the citizens to carry their own weight in public affairs—protecting the environment, reducing poverty, reducing the deficit, crime, and so on."

Martha: " . . . and improving democracy. I mean, we've got a long way to go."

Bill: "Yes, maintaining and improving democracy. That's really why we teach social studies, whatever the grade level. Dictatorships come into being very easily, and democracies are rare. What I fear, and I'm more afraid of this than losing the economic race with Japan, is that most of our students don't know enough about democracy to maintain it, let alone improve it."

"You're right, Bill," Martha added. "Our students don't know enough about democracy—about majority rule and minority rights—to create a democracy if ours was to disappear. I mean, isn't that what we should be assuring with our social studies curriculum— that Vista City graduates could reproduce a democracy if necessary? Look folks, Thomas Jefferson, James Madison, Andrew Jackson, Susan B. Anthony, Abe Lincoln, and Martin Luther King, Jr. are dead and gone. We can't rely on *them* anymore. So, who will carry on the democratic tradition?"

Bill: "Exactly. Each one of our graduates should know enough about democratic principles that they could write a democratic constitution."

Ed's eyes rolled up into his head. "Come on, Bill, get real! You, too, Martha. The business of America is business, and schools are part of that business."

Bill: "If that's true, Ed, then why are you teaching U.S. history? Why are you teaching geography and critical thinking? Why are we teaching any social studies at all? Why not just teach the three Rs and some business courses and maybe a senior seminar called, 'Lining your pockets'?"

June: "This is precisely the sort of discussion I had hoped we would have. But we have got to clear this room for another meeting at 5:30. Let's pick up where we left off next time."

Marjorie: "Is it the AIDS curriculum group that's in here next?"

"Yes," June affirmed. "There also is a religious education committee, a drug education committee, and tonight the board is conducting a hearing on whether birth control information can be given out as part of the middle school health curriculum." She slumped into her chair. "I chair each of them!"

Session #2

June: "I'm glad you all could make it to this interim meeting of the social studies committee. Our next scheduled meeting isn't until the first Tuesday in November. But it dawned on me that, before then, we should spend a few minutes reflecting on the first discussion we had two weeks ago. I thought we might share with one another our afterthoughts on that meeting."

Ellen: "Afterthoughts? I think you mean after*shocks*. I couldn't believe that I sat through Ed and Bill's debate. It's interesting, but it just isn't practical in 2nd grade."

Ed: "Isn't practical?! You mean it isn't practical at the 2nd grade to know *why* you're teaching what you're teaching? That makes no sense to me, Ellen."

Marjorie: "I think you're both right and both wrong. The way I see it is that unless we know *why* we're teaching, we have no guidance on the matter of *what* to teach."

Bill: "Or *how* to teach it. If we want thoughtful citizens, then we need to plan units that get kids to think deeply about public issues. We can't just shovel information into them and expect them miraculously to become thoughtful people."

Marjorie: "Yes, what *and* how. One of the things I've been doing since we last met is looking at the literature I select for my students. I'm trying to see if it is possible for me to concentrate on the literature that builds historical understandings, knowing that this would help both Bill and Ed in the middle grades, and Martha and Louise in high school. Now, when it comes to deciding *which* historical understandings, I'm trying to zero in on literature that develops my students' idea of what democracy is."

Ellen: "What materials are you finding?"

Marjorie: "Well, I have my 4th graders study our state—its history and geography, along with getting a general picture of each of the regions of the United States. So, I'm looking for historical literature related to each region. For the Northeast, there's the Colliers' *My Brother Sam is Dead*, about the revolutionary period. My kids can read that themselves. Together we discuss it, write about the characters, and map out the region using the textbook."

June: "Yes, that's what the textbook is for. It has the maps and the facts."

Marjorie: "Then for the Southwest, there's Elting's *The Hopi Way*, most of which I read to them. And to build on the idea of diversity, they search for information about ethnic groups living in each region. I have them do this in Jigsaw-style teams of four. Each student on a team specializes in a region and learns about the others from teammates. The point is that we can shift our planning from using whatever literature happens to be in the basal reader to zeroing in on the literature that helps our kids learn geography and history."

Ed: "You're saying that this sort of planning comes about as a result of thinking about what schools are for?"

Marjorie: "Exactly, Ed. Those debates about purpose—or aim or vision or mission or whatever you want to call it—help me choose content."

Ellen: "But, Marjorie, you have the advantage of knowing all that history. I don't. My love is language—reading and writing."

Marjorie: "Me too! Don't get me wrong, Ellen. I'm not giving up language for history. But there comes a point when you have to ask yourself: Reading and writing *what*? I mean, you can't read reading or write writing. I'm saying that we can—that we must—aim our reading and writing instruction at content. Otherwise, there just isn't time in the day to get to history and geography."

June: "And to science. That makes me think that whenever we get a basal reader sales representative in the district, we ought to start asking how that particular basal helps teach history and geography and science."

Ellen: "Good idea. We ought to expect them to help us pull social studies into language instruction, especially for people like me who don't have all the resources in mind. In the meantime, maybe Marjorie would give an inservice. She could share her plan."

Marjorie: "Ugh. Alright. But let's explore this further. Louise, what do you do with literature in your advanced placement history course in the 11th grade?"

"Well," Louise stammered, "the literature is handled by the 11th grade English teacher. I've got so much regular history to cover, you know."

June: "Yes, but we're trying to figure out how to bring them together."

Ed: "It has been a pretty simple matter for me in the 8th grade since I teach a two-hour language/history block. We read one piece of historical fiction for each era of U.S. history I cover, starting with Fast's *April Morning* for the 'shot heard 'round the world.' It's great. The kids can really relate to it."

Louise: "What's the fuss about fiction? My students read plenty, so what they need from me is a solid preparation for the AP history exam, which I can assure you does not test historical fiction or other literature."

Martha: "But it's not a matter of teaching to a test, is it? I mean, is that why you went into teaching? To find out what's on tests and then teach only that material? What if the tests don't focus on the most important material? What if they don't incorporate higher-order thinking? I think you ought to create an additional test. You could still give the AP history exam, since they need that score for college, but you could also assess their deeper knowledge of material that you choose to emphasize.

"Anyway, the advantage of literature is that it helps students enter history imaginatively rather than just skate across its surface. When we make them skate, they remember only a fraction of it and understand practically none of it."

Louise: "Well, we tried that years ago and found it didn't work."

Martha: "Tried what?"

Louise: "Integrating American literature and American history. It drove us crazy trying to do the cross-subject planning, and there weren't enough books for everyone. So they were sharing, and then a share partner would be absent and keep the book at home, and . . . ."

Martha: "Oh, that's just the 'old wine in new bottles' complaint, Louise. Like me, you know better than you teach. We all do. Our teaching is a compromise made in the face of a zillion pressures, some external, some internal. So we shouldn't sit here and justify what we do now. What we do now isn't a suitable professional standard. It's not standard setting."

Ellen (now eyeing June disapprovingly): "Martha's right. The district's testing program has got us slaving over reading and mathematics. Without some 'new wine,' we're not going to get these teachers to pay any attention to the social studies curriculum."

June: "I agree, Ellen. But are we sure that the integration of literature into the social studies program is the basket we want for all our eggs? Will it really help with the coverage problem?"

Louise: "What coverage problem? I manage to cover 500 years."

Martha: "And I cover even more than that in world history. But that's the problem. *Covering* material doesn't mean a thing."

Louise: "How can you say that?"

Martha: "Coverage doesn't mean anything in terms of what our students are *learning*. It only refers to what we are *teaching*. The problem for me is that I cannot decide what to leave out. The Egyptians? The Greeks? I just couldn't live with myself if I cut out the Roman Empire. So, I leave them in, along with everybody else: the Babylonians, Chinese, all Vikings, African civilizations, Mayans, Aztecs, Old Stone Age, New Stone Age, the agricultural revolution, the world wars, the Holocaust, Vietnam, and then there's the Feudal system, the Enlightenment, the Space Age . . . ."

Ellen: "Good grief. I can't imagine that your students can learn all of that."

Martha: "Precisely the point, Ellen. They can't. But I feel guilty when I leave a whole civilization out of the picture!"

Bill: "Perhaps we should try to help teachers in both the lower and higher grades know what to leave in and what to leave out of the social studies curriculum. When we look at the current social studies curriculum guide, you'll find that it looks like it was written by a committee. That's because it was. *Nothing* was left out, everybody's pet topic is there. I think it's impossible to teach to that guide. A teacher is forced, just by the great number of topics, to 'skate over the surface,' as you say. The kids aren't really digging into anything. I'll bet they're not remembering any of it."

June: "Well, we've raised another couple of issues: integrating history and literature, and reducing the number of topics we try to cover by planning for in-depth study. Please think some more about these before the next meeting. And we'll take up where we left off today."

Thinking About the Case

These are two sessions of a curriculum renewal committee. They are composites of actual sessions that I have observed or participated in. Both are deliberations about the social studies curriculum, so it should be helpful to analyze them, to examine what was and was not said. Reflecting in this way helps to clarify the work before such a committee, the kinds of issues that will need attention, and some of the values and goals that may be brought to that work. In fact, the first objective of curriculum renewal is to encourage thoughtful discussion—deliberation—about the curriculum, not to move mechanically through a series of steps. Thus, the following analysis is an example of one way to encourage this sort of thoughtfulness. It brings in multiple lenses through which the case can be viewed. Each adds an array of details to consider.

What Issues Were Raised?

Figure 3.1 lists the issues that I believe were raised in this case Readers may want to add issues of their own.

Figure 3.1
Issues Raised in the Case

1. Parental involvement. What kind? How? When?
2. Is expertise needed to renew a curriculum?
3. Which curriculum renewal procedures should be used?
4. Who has the authority to make curriculum decisions?
5. Should we begin or end our planning with evaluation of the existing curriculum?
6. What are the curriculum alternatives?
7. What is our aim?
8. Is pedagogy inherently political?
9. Should we develop a curriculum for which materials selection will be difficult?
10. How does commitment to a particular aim influence how and what we teach? That is, is it "practical" to discuss aims?
11. How should literature and social studies be integrated?
12. How can we set social studies firmly in the primary grades?
13. Should a curriculum set high standards for teaching or only for learning?
14. Is in-depth study on a limited number of topics better than broad coverage? Are there exceptions to this rule?
15. What kind of people do we want our students to become?

Making Sense of These Issues

Curriculum deliberation should take into account four components: subject matters, teachers, students, and milieux or contexts (organization of the school, community norms, social forces). Joseph Schwab (1970) called these components *commonplaces*. They are part of the natural terrain of curriculum planning; they come with the territory. Schwab recommends that one or more members of the committee act as representatives of each so that none will be ignored.

In Figure 3.2, I have grouped the 12 issues into the four commonplaces. Issues that, in my judgment, clearly overlap two commonplaces are placed in both groups.

Figure 3.2

Issues Grouped by Commonplaces

Subject Matters:
- What are the curriculum alternatives?
- How should literature and social studies be integrated?
- How can we set social studies firmly in the primary grades?
- Is in-depth study on a limited number of topics better than broad coverage? Are there exceptions to this rule?

Teachers:
- How can we set social studies firmly in the primary grades?
- How does commitment to a particular aim influence how and what we teach? That is, is it "practical" to discuss our aim?
- Should a curriculum set high standards for teaching or only for learning?

Students:
- What kind of people do we want our students to become?

Milieux:
- Parental involvement. What kind? How? When?
- Who has the authority to make curriculum decisions?
- What is our aim?
- Should we develop a curriculum for which materials selection will be difficult?
- How can we set social studies firmly in the primary grades?
- Is pedagogy inherently political?

Issues 2, 3, and 5 were not grouped in Figure 3.2 because they concern the renewal process itself. They compose an important fifth group of issues, planning. If the nature of curriculum planning itself is not discussed, renewal efforts will likely succumb to an array of pitfalls and bad habits (see Chapter 4). In other words, it *is* practical to think about the renewal process itself.

Only one issue was placed under the category of students. Does this mean that the sessions were weak? Should each session of a curriculum renewal effort deal with all four, now five, commonplaces? I think not. Different sessions may concentrate on just one or two of them, but it is important that all commonplaces be considered. Each brings forward a unique array of details along with a fundamental perspective on curriculum renewal.

Consider the error of not taking into account students' experiences and abilities as an integral part of decision making on subject matters. There are many reasons why students must be taken into account, but perhaps the most compelling is that the school's mission, learning, cannot be planned without figuring in students—who they are, how they make sense, what they value, what they understand and misunderstand, and what they can learn at this point in the evolution of their knowing. An excerpt from Wigginton's (1972) *The Foxfire Book* makes this clear.

> The kid who had scorched my lectern had been trying to tell me something. He and his classmates, through their boredom and restlessness, were sending out distress signals—signals that I came perilously close to ignoring.
>
> It's the same old story. The answer to student boredom and restlessness (manifested in everything from paper airplanes to dope) maybe—just maybe—is not stricter penalties, innumerable suspensions, and bathroom monitors. How many schools . . . have dealt with those students that still have fire and spirit, *not* by channeling that fire in constructive, creative directions, but by pouring water on the very flames that could make them great?

The point I want to make is that learning is a constructive activity, not a passive one, and while the teacher is the contractor, it is the students who are the laborers, the builders and assemblers of understandings. Consequently, their present understandings, cultural and linguistic identities, circumstances, habits, experiences, and abilities cannot be ignored if the school's mission is to be achieved. This is why subject matter experts—a local history professor or geographer, for example—are not always the most helpful curriculum writers. They can advise on essential learnings that need to be in the curriculum, but they may very well lack needed knowledge of students—*local* knowledge of *these* students—with which subject matter concerns must be joined. (As well, they predictably lack the needed *pedagogical* knowledge that helps transform the subject matters into material suitable and palatable for these students and this milieu [Shulman 1987].) Counselors, on the other hand, may know a great deal about these students, but may be of little help deciding on essential subject matters.

The intersection of these two commonplaces, students and subject matters, can be difficult to maneuver. It requires sustained attention. I have seen the matter degenerate to three clichés:

Question: What subjects do you teach?

Answer #1: I don't teach subjects. I teach students.
Answer #2: I don't teach subjects. I teach thinking processes so that my students can learn about any subject they want.
Answer #3: Whoever the students are, they deserve the best content; so I teach all of them Greek drama and Enlightenment philosophy.

The first cliché supports decisions to ignore subject matters for students in an attempt to "meet students' needs." In this scenario, which I find all too often among people who specialize in teaching reading and writing skills, the key educational question, Which knowledge is of most worth?, is all but forgotten. (Question: *What* do you have your students read and write about? Answer: Whatever interests them.)

More destructive than this is the use of the same cliché to justify teaching children from ghettos and impoverished rural communities only what they "need" to be marketable as skilled workers. Such a justification undergirds tracking, which denies equal access to knowledge, producing factory workers, on one hand, and scientists, on the other, at an early age.

The second cliché is often framed in the rhetoric of the "information age," a notion popularized by Alvin Toffler (1980). Several societies are entering a postindustrial age in which information is produced so rapidly that no one can possibly "know" much of it or predict what information might be needed to solve future problems. Consequently, education's emphasis should shift, the argument goes, from helping students learn specified content to increasing their ability to gather and work with—to process and think about—information.

The gaping hole in this proposition, of course, is that "processing" is treated independently of content knowledge. Actually, cognitive processing varies considerably with the subject-matter challenge at hand (Resnick 1987). As a rule of thumb, the teaching of thinking skills should pervade, not be isolated from, instruction on particular subject matter.

The third cliché can support the sort of curriculum and instruction that resulted in the scorching of Mr. Wigginton's lectern—curriculum and instruction that fail to connect subject matters meaningfully to students' lived experiences. It is in the direction of this cliché that the core curriculum movement errs if it does not overcome its Eurocentrism. Its admirable intent to expose *all* students to important learnings can become a disabling suppression of the rich individual and cultural experiences of a diverse student population (Ogbu 1990). This happens in social studies when American history is studied narrowly through the eyes and ears of a European colonizer (Banks 1988). America is thus a "New World," discounting the experience of its indigenous peoples for whom it was hardly new! Furthermore, America is "discovered" rather than settled or invaded, and when the newcomers moved from the east coast toward the west, it is known as "Westward Expansion" rather than as "The Europeans are Coming." *Care*, then, is the watchword in curriculum deliberation—care that subject matter is not used to smother one group's experiences beneath another's, care that the central curriculum question, Which knowledge is of most worth?, is paired with another: *Whose* knowledge?

This example is only one indication of the critical importance of considering all five commonplaces in curriculum deliberation. Let us look at another. It is concerned less with curriculum planning in a multicultural society than with the psychology of learning.

Not only must students' cultural identities and circumstances be intersected with subject matters, so must their growing ability to understand their world. Specifically, their ability to understand an idea should be intersected with a hierarchical plan for teaching that idea. This would not be necessary if learning was simply the accumulation of information on a topic. If that were true, a teacher would only need to determine which information students need (or let them decide) and set about exposing them to it. But it is not true.

Rather, as we have noted, learning is the progressive construction of understandings. While an understanding of some topic cannot be obtained without information, information alone will not suffice. (We can commit the Bill of Rights to memory without having the foggiest idea what these rights are or the constitutional problems they solved.) Consequently, the planning of any curriculum will need to take into account not only *which* understandings students must develop (this is the primary question), but also the *level* of understanding that will be sought at different grades (this is the subsequent question). Put differently, the committee will need to plan both scope *and* sequence.

Take, for example, the idea of *culture*. It holds a prominent position in virtually every written curriculum I have seen, but it easily falls between the cracks of the taught curriculum. One of the reasons for this is that the written curriculum does not specify an across-grade sequence of learnings that would add up to a reasonably mature understanding of this concept. Let me sketch just one approach. It is an admittedly conservative approach because learnings that could begin in earlier grades are held to later grades. A committee might be wise to err in this direction, however, because it creates a sequence that is plainly workable—one that does not invite the complaint that "my students aren't ready for this yet." Of course, good teachers will do what they've always done: teach more sophisticated understandings earlier.

Beginning in the primary grades, values related to cultural diversity should be taught directly. At the heart of these values are not just toleration, which is helpful but unambitious, but respect and appreciation, cooperation and inclusion: "People are different, and that's good." It is critical that all the adults in the school building are living examples of these values, and that they expect success from all children and interact with them accordingly. Since these values cannot be taught in the abstract, children should be introduced to interesting differences in the way people live, work, and worship. This should include local ethnic differences as well as vivid examples from abroad—the Masai of East Africa, the Sherpas of Tibet, the Indians of Peru, for example.

In the 3rd grade, more content can be added. Several communities, near and far, should be studied, and their history, geography, and social contracts compared. Using an inductive strategy, such as concept formation (Parker 1988), students should note similarities and differences among the communities' languages and customs. In this way, they will form an initial concept of culture: a people's way of life, especially their language and customs.

In the 5th grade, where the full sweep of North American history should be studied, students can extend their initial understanding of culture by comparing and contrasting the cultures of several Indian groups. This should help them appreciate the cultural diversity among Indians and counter the tendency to stereotype Indians. Students can now be introduced to an additional attribute of culture, *religion*, which will enrich their comparisons among Indian groups and between Indians and the European settlers.

By the time these students study world civilizations in the 6th grade, they will already have in mind a number of examples of culture. Therefore, they will be ready to make sense of the concepts *ethnocentrism, stereotype,* and *cultural pluralism*. Their teacher should not only teach these concepts but should also prompt students to *use* them as they study world civilizations.

The 8th grade U.S. history teacher will be grateful for this well-sequenced work on culture, since it falls to this teacher to help students grapple both with the democratic social contract *and* with the culture conflicts that abound in "a nation of immigrants." The 10th grade world history teacher will be grateful, too, because the Holocaust, racism, and apartheid are already difficult topics without having to start from scratch on the meaning of culture.

My point in this second example of intersecting commonplaces is that the committee must consider students' developing intellects and growing knowledge in relation to the essential learnings. The committee is planning not only scope but sequence. It is the latter, sequence, that cannot be considered well without taking into account the way learning actually is accomplished: Students construct their understandings gradually, adding layer upon layer, continually elaborating and refining, sometimes rebuilding previous layers and thereby shifting the very foundations of an understanding.

This is where the new California social studies framework (1988) goes wrong. In the name of in-depth study, it divides the chronological study of U.S. history roughly into thirds. The first third, covering the pre-Columbian era through the American Revolution, is placed in the 5th grade; the second third, U.S. growth and conflict (1783-1914), is placed in the 8th grade; and the final third, 1900 through the present, is in the 11th grade. This "thirding" of U.S. history is *not* to be confused with in-depth study. Rather, it practically guarantees that only superficial understandings will be developed. Why? Because it helps students develop only an initial level of understanding of each third. True in-depth study, as we will see in Chapter 6, requires students to revisit the same material, progressively working to correct misconceptions and construct a deeper and more elaborate understanding.

* * *

The case study raised many issues, making obvious the need for an analytic tool with which a committee can reflect on its deliberations and keep its collective eye on the whole terrain. It is a good idea if one or more committee members represent each of the commonplaces, speaking up when one is being ignored and serving to remind the committee of the big picture.

References

Banks, J.A. (1988). *Multiethnic Education: Theory and Practice*, 2nd ed. Newton, Mass.: Allyn & Bacon.

California State Board of Education (1988). *History-Social Science Framework*. Sacramento, Calif.: California State Department of Education.

Ogbu, J.U. (1990). "Overcoming Racial Barriers to Equal Access." In *Access To Knowledge: An Agenda For Our Nation's Schools*, edited by J.I. Goodlad and P. Keating. New York: College Entrance Examination Board.

Parker, W.C. March/April 1988). "Thinking to Learn Concepts." *The Social Studies* 79, 2: 70-73.

Resnick, L.B. (1987). *Education and Learning to Think*. Washington, D.C.: National Academy Press.

Schwab, J.J. (1970). *The Practical: A Language for Curriculum*. Washington, D.C.: The National Education Association.

Shulman, L.S. (1987). "Knowledge and Teaching: Foundations of the New Reform." *Harvard Educational Review* 57, 1: 1-22.

Toffler, A. (1980). *The Third Wave*. New York: Bantam.

Wigginton, E., ed. (1972). *The Foxfire Book*. New York: Doubleday.

4
Renewal Principles
and Procedures

For every complicated problem, there is a solution that is short, simple, and wrong.

H. L. Mencken

THREE PRINCIPLES SHOULD GUIDE CURRICULUM RENEWAL IN SOCIAL STUDIES. The first is that *curriculum renewal requires sustained deliberation about teachers, about what students at different levels of understanding can and should learn, and about the social conditions of schooling.* Because curriculum issues are essentially philosophic and political, and because we care deeply about them, disagreement is to be expected. It should be welcomed. Clarifying and talking through these disagreements, and reflecting now and then on the deliberation itself, is the routine work of curriculum deliberation.

Second, *curriculum renewal in a society striving to express the democratic ideal is necessarily different than curriculum renewal in totalitarian societies.* We would expect that the work of a curriculum committee in, for example, the People's Republic of China, where popular sovereignty is punished, is palpably different than the work of a curriculum planning committee in, for example, Costa Rica, Denmark, or the United States, where popular sovereignty is a birthright. In both settings, a curriculum committee must keep the milieu uppermost in mind. But only in the latter does the milieu permit—we should say *demand*—that the curriculum committee design a thought-provoking curriculum aimed at the cultivation of what Gutmann (1987) calls *deliberative* or *democratic* character.

Third, *curriculum renewal in a multicultural society should not be conducted in the same way it might in a monocultural society.* In a multicultural society, a planning committee, regardless of its own cultural biases, needs to build a curriculum that gives no quarter to ethnocentrism. More than this, it needs to plan a curriculum that helps children build elaborate understandings of the multicultural fabric of society and of the perennial seductions of racism, stereotyping, and prejudice. Especially now, as minority populations in the United States grow quickly and racism appears to be on the increase (Molnar 1989), the committee must not lose sight of the multicultural milieu in its deliberations.

With these principles in mind, let us consider a specific set of renewal procedures. The disadvantage of any renewal model is that it is necessarily a blunt instrument. It is too general to fit the circumstances and eccentricities of a particular renewal situation. However, the model presented here, which is adapted from Glatthorn (1987), can provide a background against which local procedures can be examined and refined.

A Renewal Model

The primary strength of this model is its naturalistic perspective. Unlike the famed curriculum development model of Ralph Tyler, to which June refers at the beginning of the case study in Chapter 3, this model is realistic. It recognizes that most social studies committees already have before them a social studies curriculum. The task, then, is less the development of a new curriculum than renewing an existing one—improving, fine tuning, or redirecting it.

The model also recognizes that there are three curriculums in each school or school district, not one. There are the recommended curriculum, the written curriculum, and the taught curriculum. The *recommended curriculum* is an ideal curriculum. A variety of individuals and groups have recommended ideal curriculums in social studies (see Chapter 5). These are critically important resources; they provide guidance and high standards for the committee's work and are grounded in sharply different philosophies of education. The *written curriculum* is the set of documents that tells a teacher, parent, or principal what students are supposed to learn. It is the formal, official curriculum. A scope-and-sequence chart, curriculum guidelines, and unit and grade level plans typically compose the written curriculum. The *taught curriculum* is what teachers actually teach. When the classroom door closes, the teacher becomes the curriculum. Period. Teachers know this well. As Martha indicated in Chapter 3, many teachers ignore the written curriculum, and many teachers, both good and bad, state proudly that they do not refer to it in their lesson planning and would be unable even to locate a copy of it.

The model I present here (Figure 4.1) strives for a consensus curriculum that brings these three curriculums, especially the written and taught, into congruence. It does this by beginning with an evaluation of the existing social studies curriculum, which involves teachers in every building. At a later point, teachers are asked to interpret proposed subject-matter themes at their grade level or, for secondary teachers, in the courses they teach.

Moreover, the model recognizes that many important learnings cannot be incorporated into the set of essential learnings identified by the renewal committee. That is, teachers and parents both want students to learn and grow more than can reasonably be expected within the essential curriculum. Trying to include all important learnings is a chief reason why the gap between the written and taught curriculums is so great. For this reason, the essential curriculum includes only a limited number of agreed-upon learnings that all students must tackle. The resources of the school and, to some extent, the home and community, are directed primarily at these learnings.

Figure 4.1
The Renewal Process

1. Evaluate the existing social studies curriculum.
2. Identify essentials that are falling through the cracks.
3. Draw the boundaries of the renewal project.
4. Educate committee members on available materials and curriculum alternatives.
5. Identify the subject-matter strands that will be threaded across the K-12 social studies curriculum.
6. Ask teachers to map the strands.
7. Collate and critique the results of mapping.
8. Plan standard-setting assessments.

Planning for these learnings includes teachers at every grade so that incipient notions developed in earlier grades can be matured into rich understandings in later grades. Selection of materials and personnel as well as assessment efforts are directed primarily at these learnings.

The model also recognizes that teachers will teach to more than these essential learnings. They will still nurture children's self-esteem; their creativity; and virtues like curiosity, honesty, and persistence; even if these are not identified as essential learnings. In other words, teachers will continue to bring their unique topics, passions, and materials into the curriculum even as they teach to the essential curriculum.

It is best not to think of the eight parts of this renewal process as steps, since steps typically are taken in order. While these eight parts are presented here in an order, the renewal process in reality involves much backtracking and looping around. Indeed, the committee should seriously consider skipping ahead to Part 8 after deliberating at Part 2. At Part 2, the committee discusses essential learnings. At Part 8, the committee concentrates on standard-setting targets for learning and instruction. Parts 2 and 8, therefore, make a natural pair, and they can be followed by returning to Parts 3 through 7, where deliberation should be aided by the preceding work at Part 8. Finally, Part 8 can be visited a second time, now for revision and elaboration.

Part 1. Evaluate the Existing Social Studies Curriculum

It is important to study the existing written curriculum and compare it to the existing taught curriculum. One way to begin is to assemble the written curriculum and to discuss it *vis a vis* the committee members' own experiences of the taught curriculum. However, this discussion needs at some point to be augmented with information from the teachers at large. The committee might provide teachers with copies of documents pertinent to the written social studies curriculum for their grade or subject and ask them to compare these with the social studies they actually teach. The committee must also find out how elementary school teachers manage to work social studies into their busy day. A memo like the one in Figure 4.2, sent to all faculty by school principals, might solicit support for this process.

Figure 4.2

I am writing to you on behalf of the district's Social Studies Curriculum Renewal Committee, which has been formed to consider how our social studies curriculum might be improved. The committee wants to involve you throughout the effort, beginning now. The first thing they need to know is what our students are currently being taught in social studies. Consequently, I am asking you to share with others, at the next faculty/departmental meeting, a brief description of the social studies topics you teach. It is important to the committee's work that you be completely frank. Please use the attached form. The meeting has been scheduled for [date].

The committee might ask building-level committees to help collate the results.

Now the committee has at least a rough idea of the taught curriculum to which it can compare the written curriculum. The committee might now assemble an Essential Learnings in Social Studies Advisory Board, described in Chapter 2. This board should be provided with the written curriculum and the collated results of the teacher survey. It can conduct other inquiries as needed. Its task, we should remember, is to advise the committee. This is best accomplished if the advisory board presents an evaluation of the existing curriculum with recommendations for its renewal at the conclusion of its studies.

The committee now has much to talk about. It has the teachers' descriptions of the taught curriculum, the advisory board's report, and its own comparison of the written and taught curriculums. As this discussion proceeds, issues, problems, and options are raised. This is helpful. (It is not "too early.") Yet, care should be taken to avoid settling on any solutions at this point, especially since alternatives have not yet been examined.

Part 2. Identify Essentials that are Falling Through the Cracks

A helpful conversation at this point concerns the question: What learnings that you value deeply and believe are truly essential do you fear might be "falling between the cracks"[1] in the existing social studies curriculum?

---

[1]This is Grant Wiggins' phrase.

Put differently: Are we presently losing sight of the forest for the trees? The committee members might list and group their ideas and then try to decide as a group which of the items could feasibly be placed into the social studies curriculum.

Often, the learnings listed in this activity will concern the entire school curriculum and climate and, beyond this, the hopes that adults generally have for the younger generation (e.g., respecting one another, displaying creativity and curiosity, taking responsibility for the quality of life in the community). Consequently, the committee should avoid the pitfall of treating *all* the items on the list as essential learnings for the social studies curriculum.

Part 3. Draw the Boundaries of the Renewal Project

The committee will be unable to direct its deliberations unless project parameters are established. Thus, it will need to know how much money and time it has and what is expected of it. Is it expected simply to adopt materials? Or is it expected to develop a new scope-and-sequence chart? If so, why? Is there not one in place now? Is the current one in need of revision so that articulation on essential learnings between grades can be made more explicit and coherent?

I have worked with many committees that were convened to revise the social studies curriculum, only to find out later that the real expectation was simply that they "adopt" a textbook series. If materials adoption is truly all that is wanted and expected, then proceeding with a curriculum renewal process is superfluous. My recommendation, however, is that a school or school district not miss the opportunity afforded by a materials adoption decision to deliberate the existing curriculums, both written and taught.

Part 4. Educate Committee Members on Available Materials and Curriculum Alternatives

There *is* a knowledge base for curriculum renewal in social studies. Its cornerstones are the three principles identified at the beginning of this chapter. More specifically, however, committee members need to know about two kinds of resources: available curriculum materials (e.g., software, textbooks, art, music, supplemental texts, literature, maps) and alternative curriculum frameworks.

Knowledge of available curriculum materials is important because, while materials obviously should not determine the curriculum, a committee should not develop a curriculum for which materials selection and location has not been considered. Avoiding the materials problem during curriculum deliberation easily makes for trouble later: Materials selection and location become pure hell and, predictably, a huge gap exists between the written and taught curriculums. As June said in Chapter 3, the committee should dream but not hallucinate.

Knowledge of an array of recommended curriculums as well as a number of exemplary curriculum guides is worthwhile, too. This knowledge helps to broaden and enrich the deliberation. Diverse perspectives, voices, and interests are brought in; comfortable assumptions and pet solutions are challenged; the windows, so to speak, are opened. It is particularly important to get copies of social studies curriculum guidelines and projects sponsored by national professional groups (e.g., the National Council for the Social Studies and the National Council of Geographic Educators), other interest groups (e.g., the Anti-Defamation League and the Bradley Commission), and other school districts. (See appendices and the summaries in the next chapter.)

Part 5. Identify the Subject-Matter Strands that will be Threaded Across the K-12 Social Studies Curriculum

This is content selection at the broadest level—the identification of essential themes that will guide the more specific unit planning within grade levels and courses. Taken together, these strands define the social studies program, K-12. When new teachers are hired and want to know what they are to teach, these strands are the short answer to their question.

The strands need to be considered when the staff development program is planned. For example, inservice workshops in both elementary and secondary grades might concentrate on improving students' reading comprehension and writing strategies *in relation to these strands*. When transfer students are enrolled, they, with their parents, should be briefed on these essential learnings. When school librarians are cross-referencing resources, they need to feature these strands as descriptors for grade-by-grade or subject-by-subject lists of related historical fiction, primary sources, biographies, software, videos and filmstrips, and reference materials (e.g., maps and globes). How else are the libraries to be organized in a school where learning the planned curriculum is the mission?

In Chapter 1, I recommend a set of five strands and related questions. Your committee may wish to use these as a starting point; revising, adding, and omitting strands and questions as needed. I advise against adding enabling skills (e.g., reading, writing, and thinking) to the set of strands because the question still remains, "Reading , writing, and thinking about *what?*" The strands should serve as the general answer to this question.

Strands should be few in number. This will help to narrow the gap between the written and taught curriculums. One way to ensure that the written curriculum will be ignored by teachers is to list too many strands or to list strands that are too broad to be helpful. I am surprised, for example, at how often I see history and each social science discipline presented as a strand. History, sociology, anthropology, geography, economics, political science, and psychology are subject areas, not essential learnings. They are too broad to be strands and, thus, leave unanswered the question, "Which learnings are most important?"

Keeping to a manageable number of fairly narrow strands should also encourage the committee early on to confront the fact that not all knowledge worth learning can be learned in school. Only a small portion of knowledge can be treated, and it should compose a critically important core of essential learnings.

Part 6. Ask Teachers to Map the Strands

The task now is to determine how teachers will make sense of these strands, and how they might work with them. A useful procedure is to develop a one– or two-page mapping form for each strand. Each form has a summary of the strand and provides space for teachers to indicate the related learnings that could be emphasized in their grade or course. Space also should be provided for teachers to tell the committee about needed prior learning.

Figures 4.3 and 4.4 contain sample mapping forms for the strands, *democracy* and *participatory citizenship*. Note that the terms are defined and teachers are asked to share what they *could* teach about each.

Figure 4.3
Sample Mapping Form: Democracy

NAME _____ SCHOOL _____

GRADE/COURSE _____

Dear Colleague:

The social studies curriculum renewal committee has identified *democracy* as an ideal that should be taught systematically throughout grades K-12. We would like your view on how this might be accomplished.

Please read the guidelines below, which give the critical attributes of democracy, and then tell us what could be done at your grade or in your course to help students learn about democracy. You should assume that the general social studies topic of your grade/course remains the same (e.g., 3rd grade: communities near and far; 10th grade: world history).

GUIDELINES: DEMOCRACY

Democracy is a social ideal under which the United States and numerous other nations are organized. This ideal has five aims: (a) to rest rule making and enforcement upon the genuine consent of the governed ("popular sovereignty"); (b) to resolve conflicts according to written law ("rule of law"); (c) to make public policy formulation the shared task of everyone ("participatory citizenship"); (d) to protect minorities from unfair incursions by the majority ("civil rights"); and (e) to accomplish change in an orderly enough way so that democracy is not sacrificed to it.

A. HERE'S WHAT I COULD TEACH RELATED TO DEMOCRACY:

B. I COULD TEACH THIS MORE SUCCESSFULLY IF, BEFORE STUDENTS GET TO ME, THEY HAVE ALREADY LEARNED THE FOLLOWING:

Figure 4.4
Sample Mapping Form: Participatory Citizenship

NAME _____ SCHOOL _____

GRADE/COURSE _____

Dear Colleague:

The social studies curriculum renewal committee has identified *participatory citizenship* as a set of skills and dispositions that should be spiraled across grades K-12. We would like your view on how this might be accomplished.

Please read the guidelines below, and then tell us what could be done at your grade or in your course to help students learn to be participating citizens.

GUIDELINES: PARTICIPATORY CITIZENSHIP

Participatory citizenship is essential in a society that is organized under the democratic ideal because democracies rely on the people themselves to participate by judging would-be representatives, deliberating controversial public issues, and sharing in the formulation of public policy. Furthermore, under the democratic ideal, all this has to be done without discrimination or repression.

The curriculum committee is particularly hopeful that students can learn to participate in disciplined discussions of public issues, since this is the most basic form of participatory citizenship. It is central to all the activities described above. Such discussions require an important issue drawn from history, current affairs, or classroom life, and the willingness and ability to listen to all voices, to clarify, and to express and support one's position.

A. HERE'S WHAT I COULD TEACH RELATED TO PARTICIPATORY CITIZENSHIP:

B. I COULD TEACH THIS MORE SUCCESSFULLY IF, BEFORE STUDENTS GET TO ME, THEY HAVE ALREADY LEARNED THE FOLLOWING:

Quality discussion time should be provided for teachers to think about the task and discuss their ideas with one another. Teachers might be asked to complete the mapping form before attending a discussion on that strand in a faculty meeting (for elementary grades) or departmental meeting (in secondary grades). Teachers should bring materials to the discussion, including lesson plan books, textbooks, workbooks, primary sources, and favorite biographies of leading democrats such as Madison, Jefferson, Whitman, Sojourner Truth, Susan B. Anthony, Martin Luther King, Jr., and so on. In an era when faculty/department meetings are easily given over to "administrivia" or to staff development related to instructional techniques, a meeting about the *curriculum* can be lively and informative. Moreover, it is immediately relevant to the school's mission: learning.

Part 7. Collate and Critique the Results of Mapping

It should be helpful to regard the process of mapping the strands as a committee-led research project, the results of which will be used to revise the strands, if needed, and to deliberate on a justifiable sequence of learnings for each strand. Teachers, of course, will differ in their treatment of a strand, so the committee will need to make decisions. The product will be an initial, tentative scope-and-sequence chart. In collating the forms, it is helpful to ask:

1. What essential strand-related learnings have been omitted that should be included?

2. What less essential content has been included that should be omitted?

3. Does the strand show desirable development from grade to grade? For example, will the sequencing give students a rich understanding of the evolution and varieties of democracy?

Part 8. Plan Standard-Setting Assessments

Now the committee should create one or two assessment items for each strand or combination thereof. This is discussed in some detail in Chapter 6, but let me say here that inventive thinking about assessment at this point should help to sharpen the conception of each strand in such a way that the scope-and-sequence chart developed in Part 7 and the strands identified in Part 5 might need to be revised.

The key question in this part of the renewal discussion is this: What kinds of things might students reasonably be expected to do before graduation to *demonstrate* a rich understanding of a strand? Of course, this question is controversial, and it is difficult enough that reasonable people will (dis)agree today and change their minds tomorrow.

One of the assessment items that I recommend for the 12th grade is answering the same questions asked on the citizenship test given to immigrants seeking U.S. citizenship. Another is a written analysis, with a map, of an international conflict. Students should know well in advance that they will be held accountable for this knowledge, thus encouraging them to direct and monitor their own learning.

Following the identification of assessment items for the 12th grade, related items should be created for benchmark assessments that occur at the end of the junior high or middle school years, and perhaps at the end of elementary school. Each of these should build logically toward the 12th grade assessment, providing feedback for students, parents, teachers, and curriculum planners on students' evolving understandings. Most important, they should provide standard-setting targets for students' schoolwork and teachers' instruction.

Pitfalls in Curriculum Renewal

I have seen five specific pitfalls often enough in my work to judge them as fairly common. The first four are essentially mistakes. Mistakes can sometimes be avoided. The fifth is a bad habit that can impede deliberation. Unlike mistakes, bad habits are difficult to avoid and can be overcome only after much time and work, but action can be taken to control their damage.

Four Mistakes

No Deliberation. Chief among the mistakes is the failure to deliberate—to hold authentic conversations on educational issues about which the participants care deeply. These are often issues on which participants disagree, so deliberation is naturally both thoughtful *and* lively. If deliberation never really occurs, then the process degenerates to a bureaucratic ritual—motion masquerading as change.

Great Plan, No Materials. A second pitfall is the failure of committee members to acquaint themselves with available materials before creating the curriculum scope-and-sequence chart. The consequence of this mistake is a sort of domino effect: The task of gathering materials to fit the new curriculum is difficult; the district does not have the resources to do the task well; the task falls to teachers whose daily schedules are already jammed; and the default condition prevails: inertia. Secondary teachers continue to teach the same curriculum they have been teaching; elementary teachers, with some notable exceptions, continue to sacrifice social studies to reading and mathematics.

Not Setting Priorities. A third mistake is the failure to identify essential content. The forms this mistake usually take are (a) identifying too many strands, (b) identifying strands that are too broadly defined (e.g, "history," "economics"), (c) identifying no strands.

Leaving the Students Out. Here I do not mean that students should be involved in content selection. But they should not be left out of the planning for their own *learning*. This mistake is nearly guaranteed to occur when assessment items are not planned at the time of curriculum renewal. Students need to know for what learnings they will be held accountable. Without this knowledge, they are left out of the planning for what is, after all, *their* learning.

...And a Bad Habit

Deliberation is at once easy and difficult. The human mind naturally questions, examines, compares, and evaluates—all the stuff of curriculum deliberation. However, it also gives in, quite readily, to all sorts of impulses that can inhibit deliberation. Perhaps the most common is the **rush to pet solutions** (Roby 1985). Consider the solutions that were raised in the case study. In-depth study was raised as a potential solution to the problem of superficial exposure to too many topics; integrating literature and social studies was raised as a solution to the problem of history being crowded out of the curriculum.

Raising a possible solution should not be confused with *rushing* to a pet solution. Rushing to a pet solution occurs when an option is raised and quickly embraced, foregoing scrutiny. Since the tensions and ambiguities that naturally accompany teaching and curriculum planning entice us toward pet solutions, this habit is prevalent. It is wise, therefore, to be ready for it. One technique is to "slow the rush" by considering a pet solution in light of the four commonplaces: subject matters, students, teachers, and milieux. By doing this—by spotting a rush to a solution, and then running it through the commonplaces—the appearance of the habit is used as a reminder to practice the art of deliberation. As one observer put it (Roby 1985, p. 24), "Having impulsively skipped ahead, (we) must artfully skip back . . . ." We skip back to appreciating in greater detail and from different perspectives the problem that the pet solution is intended to solve.

Dashing to a pet solution is often fueled by a grand theory of some sort. Proponents of an innovation will marshal evidence and mount arguments to the effect that the innovation is applicable across a remarkably wide range of situations, that it is universally effective, and, thus, that it is *the* solution to nearly any problem teachers might face. It becomes a tempting panacea promising eternal spring—motivated students, lively teaching, rapid student achievement gains, whatever. The wonders of the whole-language approach to literacy education are often expounded in this way; so are those of global education, integrated education, mastery learning, and teaching critical thinking. Each of these has considerable merit, but surely none will usher in a Golden Age. Each, we can be sure, will create problems as well as solve them.

Pet solutions can be less grand than this, simply routines that have served us well in the past and, therefore, come quickly to mind when a novel problem is encountered. Whether grand or not, pet solutions should be watched closely. As Roby (1985, p. 24) states:

> From the viewpoint of practical reasoning, skipping ahead to a solution is not *per se* an undesirable movement. Often we hit on possible solutions early in the deliberative process. What shortcircuits the process is the *love* of the solution, which unreflectively forces premature closure.

* * *

This eight-part curriculum renewal model acknowledges inevitable gaps between the recommended, written, and taught social studies curriculums. It emphasizes narrowing the gap, especially between the written and taught curriculums. The chief means for accomplishing this is deliberation among the committee members. These professional dialogues are the committee's best defense against the renewal process degenerating to a tedious bureaucratic ritual: motion without meaning or commitment.

References

Glatthorn, A.A. (1987). *Curriculum Renewal*. Alexandria, Va.: Association for Supervision and Curriculum Development.

Molnar, A. (October 1989). "Racism in America: A Continuing Dilemma." *Educational Leadership* 47, 2: 71-72.

Roby, T.W. (1985). "Habits Impeding Deliberation." *Journal of Curriculum Studies* 17, 1: 17-35.

5
Goals, Issues, and Trends

In our time, two great institutions in this country educate the young: the public schools and television. Television is, I believe, destructive not only of our sense of history but of the democratic process itself. Theoretically, television should make us better informed; in practice we are rendered numb and dumb. Theoretically, it should extend our knowledge of the world; in reality, it narrows our vision . . . . History in the schools could exert a major countervailing force to this omnipresent educator.

—Hazel W. Hertzberg

WHAT DOES THE TYPICAL K-12 SOCIAL STUDIES CURRICULUM LOOK LIKE? What are some prominent alternatives? With what issues is the field grappling, and what trends will shape the coming years? My answers to these questions, drawn from research[1] and personal observations, are the content of this chapter. (Three of the social studies curriculum guides referred to in this chapter are excerpted in the appendices of this book.)

Controversy Comes with the Territory

We need to understand that social studies curriculum planning is inherently controversial. Social studies involves many hot topics that are hot precisely because people care deeply about them: values, religion, loyalty, patriotism, authority, peace, property, privacy,

---

[1]For helpful literature reviews, see Morrissett 1982 and Shaver, Davis, and Helburn 1979.

justice, capitalism and socialism, business and labor, ethnic and national identities. Committee members, community groups (including parents), and teachers will find many issues to debate.

Community Groups

Consider again the issues raised in the case study presented in Chapter 3. Many of them are what we might call "in-house" controversies, the kind that school people debate but that parents and interest groups in the community may overlook. Parents and interest groups are likely to raise different questions, such as:

• **Should children work together in so-called "cooperative groups"? Doesn't this hold the brighter students back?** These are important questions. So-called cooperative learning techniques, such as Jigsaw (Slavin 1986), are promising ways to increase not only social skills but *learning* in social studies.

• **Why are you teaching Islam and Buddhism? We are mostly Christians here.** Some parents are uninformed about education on world religions, failing to distinguish between the teaching *of* religion, as in "Sunday school," and teaching *about* religion, which is a vitally important aspect of a history course.

• **What is "social studies" anyway? Where did history and geography go?** It is helpful to clarify for parents that the term *social studies* is jargon among educators for history, geography, and civics.

• **Whose values are being promoted in the social studies curriculum?** Values most definitely are being promoted in the social studies curriculum. This cannot be avoided. It is important, therefore, to identify and clarify the values that are emphasized. Also, analysis of the role of values in history should be a vital part of the social studies curriculum. Without understanding the values that motivated the Anasazi, the Pilgrims, Columbus, Madison, Sojourner Truth, or Chief Joseph, students cannot really know who these people were or why they behaved as they did.

• **Is global education a world peace movement? Don't kids have enough to learn about just in America?** Global education is a confusing term. Some parents worry that it refers to a liberal political agenda. World studies or international studies are perhaps clearer terms (Woyach and Remy 1989). Regardless of the label, this content must be a central part of the social studies curriculum. It is one of five content strands recommended in

61

Chapter 1 and includes the study of world cultural geography, world history, and international relations. Just about every social studies topic that is treated in depth, K-12, ought to incorporate an international comparison or perspective.

• **Why are so many football coaches teaching U.S. history?** Not enough parents and superintendents ask this question. Perhaps they have caved into our society's celebration of athletic challenge. We all know that schools are under great pressure from their communities to sustain a vigorous team-sports program (not to be confused with a vigorous physical/health education program). It is well-known, too, at least among school teachers, that applicants for teaching positions who will coach after-school sports are often given priority over applicants who will not.

This question thus returns us to the issue of the school's mission (discussed in Chapter 2). Why has athletic competition been enthroned in our schools? To what extent will we permit it further to undermine academic learning?

Teachers

Classroom teachers, too, will disagree in their advice to the curriculum committee, in part because of their diverse priorities. Some teachers are *special topic enthusiasts*, inclined to spend much of the available instructional time teaching the topic they know and love. Here we find the Civil War buff, the China specialist, the women's studies enthusiast, or the teacher for whom "social studies" means map and globe skills.

Others are *skills enthusiasts*. They emphasize writing skills, thinking skills, reading and study skills, or others, in the hope that, with these well in hand, students can learn *any* content. Still other teachers give top priority to the development of students' *self-esteem*. Whatever content and skills are specified in the written curriculum, these teachers will subordinate them to building students' sense of competence and worth (Newmann 1986).

Hence, the planning committee is wise to expect and welcome controversy. It should respond by working toward consensus, keeping its sights on narrowing the gap between the written and taught curriculums.

A National Pattern

In spite of the ample opportunities for controversy within school districts, and the large number of school districts (about 16,000) making their own social studies curriculums, there is, in effect, a national social studies scope and sequence, as shown in Figure 5.1 (Morrisett 1982).

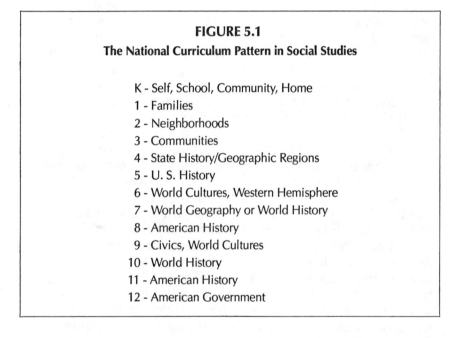

FIGURE 5.1

The National Curriculum Pattern in Social Studies

K - Self, School, Community, Home
1 - Families
2 - Neighborhoods
3 - Communities
4 - State History/Geographic Regions
5 - U. S. History
6 - World Cultures, Western Hemisphere
7 - World Geography or World History
8 - American History
9 - Civics, World Cultures
10 - World History
11 - American History
12 - American Government

The name often given to the K-6 portion of this dominant scope-and-sequence pattern is *expanding environments* or *expanding horizons*, and it is followed by two cycles of *contracting environments* (7-9, 10-12). Of course, the one- and two-word descriptors given for each grade in this scope-and-sequence pattern tell us very little about the specific content that is selected in each of these grades, not to mention what actually gets taught.

What accounts for this uniformity across the school districts? Here are my three hunches: First, this scope-and-sequence chart makes sense to teachers. Teachers of young children are well aware of their students' limited knowledge, so it seems perfectly reasonable to begin with what the children already know to some degree—people and places in their immediate environment—and move gradually outward to the less familiar and the more abstract—people like James Madison, Sojourner Truth, and Chief Joseph, and difficult geographic and political entities like continents, nations, and the Southern Hemisphere. Of course, we know that children can and do grasp their world in a more complex way than this, but, still, the expanding environments pattern is helpful as a curriculum organizer. It provides useful handles on what otherwise would be an enormously jumbled bundle of subject matters. The most vocal critics of the expanding environments, I have noticed, are often not people who work in schools who must continually figure out how to make content manageable for students (e.g., Ravitch 1987).

Second, because most teachers and curriculum planners themselves experienced this framework when they were students, it has, for better or worse, a "natural" feel to it.

Third, most social studies programs are based on published materials. This was the basis of June's concern in the Vista City case study. If her committee placed world history at the 4th grade, she knew very well that her teachers would have to write their own textbooks because relatively few curriculum materials are available on that subject at that grade level. World history materials are, however, plentiful for the 6th, 7th, and 10th grades. A cycle is at work here: When textbook publishers research the market to determine which books will sell at which grade levels, they find that teachers generally report they want materials that fit the current framework. Understandably, it is difficult to persuade a textbook publisher to produce a 4th grade world history text when the publisher is convinced that the sales will not justify the production cost.

There has been a good deal of controversy over the past 60 years about this K-12 scope and sequence. Perhaps it is this framework's vague quality that, like an ink blot, permits it to be interpreted in so many ways. Historians look at it, see too little history, and call for more. Meanwhile, the business community calls for more free-enterprise education (often called "economics"), geographers for more geography, political scientists for more civics, and so on. Historians and geographers especially have wanted more history and geography in the primary grades where, they argue, the expanding environments framework offers only vacuous material about community workers and cooperation—what one critic calls "tot sociology" (Ravitch 1987). This claim might be justified if we looked only at the one-word names given above for grades 1-3, or only at the titles of textbooks for these grades. But if we look *inside* we're likely to find history and geography. Consider these primary grade lessons, *Neighborhoods* and *Communities*, found in a new 2nd grade social studies textbook, *The World Around Us* (1990):

- Geography—"Following Routes on Maps," "Using a Compass Rose," and "Reading Landform Maps"
- Geography-Oriented Biography—"Sally Ride: A Person Who Saw the Earth from Space"
- History—"The First Americans" (a Powhatan Indian village), "The Jamestown Settlement," and "Pioneer Life" (each with maps)
- Historical Biography—"Paul Revere: A Person Who Helped Our Country to be Free"

It is difficult, therefore, to justify the claim that the expanding environments pattern ignores history and geography in the elementary grades. In my judgment, the criticism of this pattern is a form of scapegoating related to students' poor knowledge of history and geography, revealed vividly in recent surveys. A more likely problem is that social studies is not being taught regularly in the elementary grades.

Elementary school teachers and curriculum supervisors often do not make enough time for social studies, *whatever the particular curriculum pattern*. If history and geography are not taught, we should not be surprised that they are not learned. Blame well could be diverted from the expanding environments framework to contextual factors of the kind discussed in Chapter 2—realities that mitigate the teaching of *any* social studies. These include:

- **The personnel-selection problem**—How many teachers and their supervisors *know* history, civics, and geography?
- **The school's mission**—Is learning taken as seriously as athletic challenge? Who is promoted into administrative positions, and why? What is the content of school assemblies? The morning announcements?
- **Departmentalization of knowledge**—If reading is given so much attention in the school day, why can't children be reading history, biography, and maps?
- **The testing frenzy in basic skills**—Why is the school district satisfied to hold children accountable for reading and

mathematics skills but not for their understandings of history, civics, and cultural geography?

• **Tracking**—Which students get the most exposure to social studies knowledge? Which students get the least? Why?

Alternatives

The time and energy of curriculum planners most profitably will be spent not in seeking the "ideal" curriculum, but in seeking a sound one that will win a secure place in the curriculum. Comparing and contrasting alternative patterns is one vital method for achieving this. Several alternatives have been proposed. The National Council for the Social Studies (NCSS) recommends three that are excerpted in the appendix of this book: One is based on the expanding environments framework and is only slightly different from the national pattern (Appendix 1). The other two are thematic: One emphasizes global education (Appendix 3); the other includes this global dimension but emphasizes "enlightened democratic citizenship" for the 21st century (Appendix 2).

Figure 5.2 lists NCSS's (1989) 24 criteria for selecting the three frameworks it recommends. The list is long. Clearly, it was conceived by a committee and few ideas were left out. Yet, reviewing it may suggest criteria for a local curriculum committee to consider as it designs and selects its framework.

Let me draw the reader's attention to two especially important criteria: internal consistency (#2) and a public issues emphasis (#21). The social studies goal known as "democratic citizenship" is easy to espouse but difficult to deliver. Any curriculum framework must be scrutinized for its potential to make good on this promise. Most, in my judgment, do not. They lack the necessary internal consistency between the goal and the scope-and-sequence plan. Criteria #21, above the rest, addresses the needed ends-means consistency.

A long line of curriculum scholarship supports my point (Dewey 1915, Evans 1989). None of the frameworks selected by NCSS emphasizes these two criteria sufficiently. Nor does the Bradley Commission's framework or the new California framework. Yet, an issue-centered K-12 social studies framework is quite feasible. I highlight it later in this chapter and again in Chapter 6. Its importance lies in overcoming the decades-old inconsistency between social studies goals and social studies practice. But first, let us look more closely at some of the alternatives to the national pattern.

FIGURE 5.2

Social Studies Scope-and-Sequence Criteria

1. State the purpose and rationale of the program
2. Be internally consistent with its stated purposes and rationale
3. Designate content at every grade level, K-12
4. Recognize that learning is cumulative
5. Reflect a balance of local, national, and global content
6. Reflect a balance of past, present, and future content
7. Provide for students' understanding of the structure and function of social, economic, and political institutions
8. Emphasize concepts and generalizations from history and the social sciences
9. Promote the integration of skills and knowledge
10. Promote the integration of content across subject areas
11. Promote the use of a variety of teaching methods and instructional materials
12. Foster active learning and social interaction
13. Reflect a clear commitment to democratic beliefs and values
14. Reflect a global perspective
15. Foster the knowledge and appreciation of cultural heritage
16. Foster the knowledge and appreciation of diversity
17. Foster the building of self-esteem
18. Be consistent with current research pertaining to how children learn
19. Be consistent with current scholarship in the disciplines
20. Incorporate thinking skills and interpersonal skills at all levels
21. Stress the identification, understanding, and solution of local, national, and global problems
22. Provide many opportunities for students to learn and practice the basic skills of participation from observation to advocacy
23. Promote the transfer of knowledge and skills to life
24. Have the potential to challenge and excite students

Perhaps the most provocative is one put forward by the Bradley Commission on History in the Schools (1988), shown in Figure 5.3.

FIGURE 5.3

Social Studies as History

K - Children's Adventures: Long Ago and Far Away

1 - People Who Made America

2 - Traditions, Monuments, and Celebrations

3 - Inventors, Innovators, and Immigrants

4 - Heroes, Folk Tales, and Legends of the World

5 - American History: Biographies and Documents

6 - World History: Biographies and Documents

7 - Local History; Electives

8 - History of European Civilization

9 - History of non-European Civilization

10 - U.S. History and Geography to 1865

11 - U.S. History and Geography since 1865

12 - American Government; Elective

Noteworthy here is the straightforward (but single-minded) history education contained in the primary grades and, in the secondary grades, the two-year sequences in world history and U.S. history. Six themes, some too broad to be helpful as content selection guides, elaborate somewhat the content at each grade level:

1. Civilization, cultural diffusion, and innovation
2. Human interaction with the environment
3. Values, beliefs, political ideas, and institutions
4. Conflict and cooperation
5. Comparative history of major developments
6. Patterns of social and political interaction

We might compare this history-dominated framework to the global education alternative found in Appendix 3. Its author leaves the planning of sequence to the local curriculum committee but proposes four "essential elements" and five "themes," which are to be spiraled through the K-12 sequence. The essential elements , listed in Figure 5.4, define global education; the themes focus attention, make connections across the curriculum, and encourage transfer of knowledge from the classroom to everyday life.

FIGURE 5.4

Social Studies as Global Education
(Kniep 1989)

Essential Elements

1. The Study of Systems
2. The Study of Human Values
3. The Study of Persistent Issues and Problems
4. The Study of Global History

Themes

1. Interdependence
2. Change
3. Culture
4. Scarcity
5. Conflict

When considering alternative curriculum patterns, it is useful to return to the ends-means problem as well as the pitfalls discussed at the end of Chapter 4. We might also remember June's comment in the first Vista City meeting: "We want to dream, but not hallucinate. We don't want to create a social studies plan for which there are no materials, or for which materials selection is so difficult that teachers will just not teach social studies." If the committee plans a curriculum for which materials are not available, one that teachers cannot understand, or one that does not seem important to them, then the default condition is likely to occur: inertia. In the elementary grades, this usually means intense instruction in reading and mathematics and little in social studies. In the secondary grades, this can mean U.S. history taught superficially without controversy or discussion, and perhaps no world history and only the weakest civics. It is this default condition that the committee should diligently work to avoid.

Goals

In addition to a national scope-and-sequence pattern, there is something of a national goals statement for social studies. The central goal of social studies is commonly given as education for democratic citizenship. School districts typically divide this goal into four parts: knowledge, skills, values, and participatory citizenship. The last of these, the most recent addition, is sometimes grouped with skills.

Knowledge

The knowledge goal is often specified as the subject areas of history and the social sciences—geography, economics, political science or civics, anthropology, sociology, and psychology. Actually, these are not knowledge goals, but *sources* of knowledge goals.

Let us look at two variations. The first of the three scope-and-sequence alternatives recommended by the National Council for the Social Studies (NCSS), the one that follows the expanding environments pattern, emphasizes that "knowledge is derived from encounters students have with the subject matter of the social studies . . . ." The "essential sources" of that subject matter "from which knowledge goals for social studies should be selected" are given as follows:

> • History—of the United States and the world; understanding change and learning to deal with it
> • Geography—physical, political, cultural, economic; world-wide relationships
> • Government—theories, systems, structure, processes
> • Law—civil, criminal, constitutional, international
> • Economics—theories, systems, structures, processes
> • Anthropology and Sociology— cultures, social institutions, the individual, the group, the community, the society
> • Psychology—the individual in intergroup and interpersonal relationships
> • Humanities—the literature, art, music, dance, and drama of cultures
> • Science—the effects of natural and physical science on human relationships

(Task Force on Scope and Sequence 1989)

A second variation on the knowledge goal comes from the California State Board of Education (1988), which says in the new *History–Social Science Framework*:

> The goal of knowledge and cultural understanding is pursued by developing students' literacy in history and the other humanities (including ethics), geography, economics, sociology, and political science. Certain essential learnings are integral to the development of each of these literacy strands.

Those essential learnings are then listed and detailed. Included are historical literacy, ethical literacy, cultural literacy, geographic literacy, economic literacy, and sociopolitical literacy.

The problem remains for teachers to make sense of the knowledge goal and transform it into lessons and units. It is helpful when the curriculum renewal committee provides examples. Let me give two, one for the 3rd grade and one for the 11th grade. Each uses the five strands recommended in Chapter 1 as aids to content selection.

Third Grade. A 3rd grade teacher, working within the broad expanding environments framework, concentrates all year on the broad concept *community*. She decides to have her students study their own local community and four others during the year. With an eye to the strand, global perspective (see Chapter 1), she identifies a community abroad that is similar in some essential way to the local community (e.g., a "sister city" abroad that is also a port). She also selects the three others, keeping in mind her own knowledge of available materials. Two of these might be early communities in North America (e.g., the Anasazi village and the Jamestown settlement). The other might be another community in the same state or a community that her students select from a list she provides.

Across this multiple-case community study, the teacher highlights the four remaining strands: She has her students learn about governance in each community and the different demands made on citizens in each; she also has them chart the similarities and differences between the pre-industrial and industrial communities and describe ethnic diversity and relations within each community. Meanwhile, to build participatory competencies, she teaches her students to conduct democratic meetings where classroom problems are discussed.

Eleventh Grade. The 11th grade U.S. history teacher decides to arrange the year's units chronologically. Both his text and his supplemental materials do this. With an eye to the five strands, he plans to emphasize the evolution and problems of democracy across United States' agricultural, industrial, and, now, postindustrial eras. He wants to highlight the nature and extent of ethnic diversity within each era and to stress the demands this places on the evolution of democracy. The status of popular sovereignty and civil liberties in two emerging democracies in Europe, Latin America, or Asia is compared to the era when democracy was first emerging in the United States. To bring these strands together meaningfully for students, while at the same time incorporating the participatory citizenship strand, the teacher isolates for discussion a controversial public issue from each era.

In both examples, we see a teacher working with a grade level's general topic ("communities" and "U.S. history") and using the five essential strands to specify content and experiences.

Skills

Skills, especially thinking skills, are very important to social studies educators. After reviewing what has been written about social studies during the 20th century, one justifiably could conclude that thinking skills are the most persistently pursued of all social studies objectives (Parker in press). As much work has been done to identify and clarify the thinking skills that teachers should teach as the knowledge they should teach.

In 1956, Benjamin Bloom's well-known *Taxonomy of Educational Objectives: Handbook 1: Cognitive Domain* popularized the distinction between lower- and higher-level thinking. The key to the lower/higher distinction is the difference between gathering and remembering information, on the one hand, and interpreting, elaborating, manipulating, and applying it, on the other. In other words, higher-order thinking requires students to *go beyond the information given* (Newmann 1988). For example, students might be required to commit to memory the conditions that lead to the rise of the Nazis in Germany, or they might be asked to learn these conditions *and* apply them to other times and places, predicting whether the conditions are right for Naziism to arise there also.

Curiously, while much attention is paid in social studies journals and conferences to teaching in ways that press students to engage in higher-level thought, research finds that *if* social studies is taught (a big "if" in the elementary grades), the methods teachers generally

72

use encourage only data gathering and memorizing. Of course, there are exceptions,[2] but they are nonetheless exceptions.

Let us look at the treatment of the skills goal in three social studies curriculum guides. In the first of the three alternatives recommended by NCSS (Appendix 1), skills are defined as "the ability to do something proficiently in repeated performances." NCSS treats them as "processes that enable students to link knowledge with beliefs that lead to action." Three categories of skills are included in that framework:

- **Skills related to acquiring information** (e.g., reading and study skills, reference and information skills)
- **Skills related to organizing and using information** (e.g., intellectual and decision-making skills)
- **Skills related to interpersonal and social participation** (e.g., personal, group interaction, and political participation skills)

The California framework gives basically the same sets of skills: basic study skills, critical thinking skills (e.g., define and clarify problems, recognize stereotypes and propaganda), and participation skills (e.g., group interaction, political participation).

The Bradley Commission on History in the Schools has a more ambitious approach to social studies skills. It recommends that studies in history, geography, and civics be designed "to take students well beyond formal skills of critical thinking" to the formation of *habits of mind* (Figure 5.5). Broader and deeper than skills, these are perspectives and ways of thinking. It is helpful to view these as inclinations or dispositions—the inclination to approach problems thoughtfully rather than impulsively, for example. So disposed, students are more likely to use whatever thinking skills they have learned. Without these inclinations, it is difficult to imagine that any amount of skills instruction would suffice. To nurture them, the commission recommends the sustained study chiefly of history—a history that illuminates vital themes and significant questions and that (returning to the essence of higher-order thinking):

---

[2]For exceptions, see my trends column in *Educational Leadership* (e.g., October 1989 and November 1987 issues contain descriptions of exceptional elementary school teachers). For secondary school exceptions see Samuel S. Wineburg and Suzanne M. Wilson. September 1988. "Models of Wisdom in the Teaching of History," *Kappan*, Vol. 70, No. 1, 50-58.

reaches beyond the acquisition of useful facts. Students should not be left in doubt about the reasons for remembering certain things, for getting facts straight, for gathering and assessing evidence. "What of it?" is a worthy question and it requires an answer.

FIGURE 5.5

History's Habits of Mind

Students are disposed to:

- Understand the significance of the past to their own lives, both private and public, and to their society
- Distinguish between the important and the inconsequential, to develop the "discriminating memory" needed for a discerning judgment in public and personal life
- Prepare to live with uncertainties and exasperating, even perilous, unfinished business, realizing that not all problems have solutions
- Appreciate the often tentative nature of judgments about the past, and thereby avoid the temptation to seize upon particular "Lessons" of history as cures for present ills

---

Values

Values are integral to the social studies curriculum. Most written social studies curriculums specify particular values that should be promoted as part of the social studies program. Values education is unavoidable because citizenship education, the central goal of social studies education, implies *good* citizenship.

What is good citizenship? Clearly, that depends on the particular social ideal under which a society has been organized. For a society like the United States, which is organized under the *democratic* ideal, good citizenship involves the values grounded in source documents such as the Declaration of Independence, the Constitution of the United States, the Bill of Rights, and more recent expressions such as the Seneca Fall's Declaration of the Rights of Women and Martin Luther King's "I Have A Dream" speech.

Consequently, a rather standard list of values appears in social studies curriculum guides: human dignity, rule by law, justice, equality, responsibility, freedom, diversity, and privacy (NCSS 1979). The first of the three curriculum recommendations found in the appendices goes further, listing 31 values grouped in four categories:

rights of the individual, freedoms of the individual, responsibilities of the individual, and beliefs concerning social conditions and governmental responsibilities.

The new California framework boils this down to two categories:

• **Understand what is required of citizens in a democracy** (e.g., taking individual responsibility for one's own ethical behavior, controlling inclinations against aggression, and attaining a certain level of civility)

• **Understand individual responsibility for the democratic system** (e.g., students need to ponder the fragile nature of the democratic system and the processes through which democracies perish)

Several means of values education have been worked out by social studies educators and psychologists, including: inculcation, analysis, clarification, action learning, and moral development (Superka et al. 1975). The first is the most widely practiced, and the last is the most widely researched (see Reimer et al. 1983 and Noddings 1984).

A curriculum guide typically does not refer to a particular means of teaching values; rather it lists the values students should somehow display. This is unfortunate for at least one reason. If democratic citizenship is the overarching mission of a social studies program, and if democracies are indeed fragile, then at least one approach to values education in social studies is essential: the *issues-oriented approach*. It is closely associated with democratic imperatives, it is feasible, and thoughtful rationales for it have been written. The issues-oriented approach to values education provides frequent and sustained opportunities for students to engage in lively discussions of pressing public issues. Further, it provides instruction on the procedures and, to a degree, on the inclinations that sustain such discussions. The issues are drawn mainly from history, but also from contemporary policy discussions—both in the school (locker searches for drugs) and the community (gun control laws)(Evans 1989).

To one degree or another, this approach to values education involves all five means listed earlier:

• **Inculcation**—In issues-oriented discussions, students are exhorted to be inquisitive listeners as well as skilled talkers, and to be well-informed on the issues.

• **Analysis**—Students are taught to bring logical thinking to the examination of public issues—to detect bias and determine the credibility of sources, to draw historical parallels, and to spend considerable time stating and clarifying issues.

• **Clarification**—Students are helped to become aware of their own values and to express them openly and honestly in discussions.

• **Action Learning**—Disciplined discussion of public issues with peers *is* action. Open, free, public talk is the most basic form of action in a democratic society.

• **Moral Development**—Students are encouraged to grow in their ability to reason in a principled way about public issues by giving reasons for their opinions and listening carefully to different lines of reasoning on the same problem.

The importance of the values component of the common four-fold expression of social studies goals (values, participation, skills, knowledge) is not only that it encourages curriculum planners and teachers to make values education an objective in every grade, unit, and course, but that the presence of this component in the guidelines reminds planners, teachers, and parents that social studies education is *not* void of values. Instead, it exists inevitably in relation to one social ideal or another. In the United States, as in many other societies, that ideal is democracy; consequently, the social studies curriculum seeks, more than anything else, to initiate students into an ongoing dialogue and inquiry on democracy, into the tradition of increasing liberty and rising hope. We want to graduate high school seniors who are capable of constituting a democratic government themselves and who will in their own lives make manifest the democratic ideal.

Participation

Of the four goals, participation has been dealt with perhaps the least. In fact, one scholar has called it "unrealistic." In reviewing Fred Newmann's exciting but difficult model for advancing this goal, Gerald Marker (quoted in Morrissett 1982) concluded that "such efforts fall of their own weight; teachers find that they cannot keep up such a pace with the typical five-class day." In Newmann's model, teachers had to make numerous arrangements to place students in community agencies, to transport them to and from school, and so on.

What exactly is this participatory citizenship goal? Essentially, it seeks to give students a kind of education that falls naturally at the intersection of time-honored pedagogical wisdom—active learning—and the overarching goal of social studies education—democratic citizenship. As spelled out in Newmann's model, this goal aims to increase students' competence to exert influence over public issues—formulating goals and winning support for them (Newmann et al. 1977). Seven specific competencies compose this goal (see Figure 5.6).

FIGURE 5.6

Participatory Competencies
(Newmann et al. 1977)

Students should be able to:

1. Communicate effectively in spoken and written language
2. Collect and logically interpret information on problems of public concern
3. Describe political-legal decision-making processes
4. Rationally justify personal decisions about controversial public issues and explicate action strategies with reference to principles of justice and constitutional democracy
5. Work cooperatively with others
6. Discuss concrete personal experiences of one's self and others in ways that contribute to resolution of personal dilemmas encountered in civic action and relate these experiences to more general human issues
7. Use selected technical skills as they are required for exercise of influence on specific issues

---

In its simplest and most profound sense, participatory citizenship is the sustained opportunity to talk frankly about pressing public issues. Public talk, as Benjamin Barber (1989) calls it, is the basic, unglamorous work of democracy—whether the talker is an average citizen or an elected or appointed representative. According to Barber, public talk is "talk in common among a community of citizens about common issues—the public good, for example." Brought down in this way from unfeasible, lofty heights (e.g., participating in a legislative or initiative campaign), this conception of participatory citizenship is readily feasible in schools, worthy, and exciting.

A number of participatory citizenship programs are underway across the United States, demonstrating that the goal is not unmanageably difficult to realize. Many are described in the October 1989 issue of *Social Education*. Perhaps the most interesting of these is the new, one-semester "participation in government" course required of 12th grade students in New York. School districts can design their own courses and, thanks to the demand from New York, several publishing houses are beginning to supply materials.

My favorite, from the National Issues Forum in the Classroom (1990-91), is an example of the issues-oriented approach to values education. Nine issue units were developed. Each unit has a booklet of readings that provides background information and a teacher's guide. The issues are not only current, they are *re*current, for example, "Immigration: What We Promised, Where to Draw the Line" and "Coping with AIDS: The Public Response to the Epidemic," and "The Battle over Abortion: Seeking Common Ground in a Divided Nation." Teachers and students are encouraged to select only four of the nine units, allowing time for in-depth study, including discussions, interviews, and field trips. The final issue unit, "Developing an Issue," takes students through the steps of identifying and defining a local issue and generating policy options.

Through this program, we see again how the issue-centered approach covers much ground. It serves not just the values education goal but the three other goals as well: participation ("public talk"), skills (needing to reason beyond the information given), and knowledge (the issues are related to the understandings we want students to develop).

Current Issues

Among the issues challenging the social studies field today are three that concern content in the primary grades, the amount of social studies required in the secondary grades, and student attitude toward social studies.

Issue #1: Should the Content of the Primary Grades Be Beefed Up?

I agree with those who want more history and geography in the primary grades, K-3. The school day in these grades easily fills up with reading, mathematics, and classroom management. Consequently, the problem of teaching more social studies is not likely to be solved by overturning the expanding environments framework. I stress this because it is the solution most often proposed. Indeed, we have seen this solution is far off the mark. (Remember, the expanding environments framework already includes history and geography.) This leads us to consider the distinction between the written and taught curriculums: In the former, history and geography are not rare; in the latter they are. Social studies *in any form* is not common in the primary grades for two reasons.

First, elementary teachers and administrators may lack knowledge of history and geography, especially the kind of knowledge needed most by educators: the pedagogical knowledge of history and geography that enables them to make these subjects meaningful and intriguing for young learners. Second, media and public officials are exerting pressure to raise scores in reading and mathematics, not social studies. Thus, the most important and difficult work of the curriculum renewal committee is to reduce the gap between the written and taught curriculums in social studies; in other words, to secure a place for social studies in the elementary school day.

Issue #2: How Much Social Studies Should Be Required in the Secondary Grades?

Electives flourished in the 1970s under three specious banners: relevance, individuality, and the notion that subject matter is unimportant since, in a post-industrial age, the processes of thinking count more than the content of thought. The trend now is to correct the content-poor curriculum that resulted, and the chief means is to replace electives with requirements in nearly all of the secondary social studies curriculums.

I welcome this trend. Too many of our high school graduates have studied virtually no world history, participated in no courses of study that developed their ability to discuss public policy questions, and possess only a thin understanding of the debates and struggles that compose U.S. history. Where tracking is practiced, this characterization especially applies to students from middle- and low-income families.

The National Commission on Social Studies in the Schools (1989), the California framework and the Bradley Commission on

History in Schools all recommend that students take at least one social studies *course* every semester, grades 7 through 12, and each of these recommendations includes only one or two social studies *electives*.

The National Commission recommends a one-semester elective in the 12th grade. The options for this elective are (1) courses in anthropology, sociology, psychology; (2) a recurrent issues course; or (3) a supervised experience in community service.

The California framework suggests two one-semester social studies electives in the 9th grade. Twelve options are recommended: 20th century state history, physical geography, world regional geography, the humanities, comparative world religions, area studies (cultures), anthropology, psychology, sociology, women in history, ethnic studies, and law-related education.

The Bradley Commission proposes a one-semester social studies elective in the 7th grade and another in the 12th.

The great bulk of study, then, is to be done in required courses. The National Commission recommends local history (grade 7), United States history (grade 8), world and American history and geography to 1750 (grade 9), world and American history and geography, 1750-1900 (grade 10), world and American history and geography since 1900 (grade 11), and a one-semester course in economics and American government (grade 12).

California recommends world history and geography in medieval and early modern times (grade 7); U.S. history and geography, from the Constitution to the World War I (grade 8); modern world history, culture, and geography (grade 10); 20th century U.S. history (grade 11); and economics and "principles of American democracy" (grade 12).

The Bradley Commission recommends local history (grade 7), European history (grade 8), non-European history (grade 9), U.S. history and geography to 1865 (grade 10), U.S. history and geography since 1865 (grade 11), and a one-semester American government course (grade 12).

Issue #3: Can Students' Attitudes Toward Social Studies Be Improved?

Research suggests that "most students in the United States, at all grade levels, find social studies to be one of the least interesting, most irrelevant subjects in the school curriculum" (Shaughnessy and Haladyna 1985). And this general dislike increases with each grade level. What's to be done? One group argues that social studies must be made more *relevant* to students' present lives, particularly their vocational interests. Another group argues that the social studies curriculum must be made more *exciting*. Another group focuses on social studies lessons, arguing that they need to become more *engaging*.

All three can help, but qualifications are needed. While social studies should be made relevant to students' lives, it is critical that we see this as an instructional goal, not a curricular one. We must not make social studies relevant by differentiating the curriculum, giving the most highly valued knowledge to only a few students (see the discussion of tracking in Chapter 2). Rather, virtually all children should have access to highly valued knowledge, which should in turn be made relevant to their lives. This is an instructional challenge of the highest order, which Dewey (1915) describes in his splendid essay, *The Child and the Curriculum*. He calls the task "psychologizing" the subject matter: The teacher is to select content worth knowing, then connect it to the child's present experience, and build from there.

It is also true that the curriculum needs to be reasonably interesting, but we shouldn't have to resort to television-style gimmicks to attract students. Here, the goal is curricular rather than instructional. The curriculum needs to be vitally important. This is a content selection issue at a level of specificity well beyond where curriculum guides typically go. The questions become *Which* history? *Which* biographies? *Which* historical fiction? *Which* maps? *Which* recurrent public issues? *Which* ethnic groups? *Which* democracies?

At this point, at least three factors seem to guide teachers' decision making about content: their intentions and goals, their knowledge of the subject matter, and their knowledge of available curriculum materials. This is where the taught curriculum is created, and its creator is the classroom teacher. In Chapter 1, I suggest five across-grade strands and give examples of how an elementary and a secondary teacher used those strands in unit planning. For a middle school example, consider the American history teacher who is convinced that her students can imaginatively enter the Civil War era. She chooses biographies as the centerpiece of the unit. Which biographies? Abraham Lincoln and Harriet Tubman are good choices along with Tutu and Mandela in South Africa. Together with explanations drawn from the textbook, these biographies can help students elaborate an understanding of democratic citizenship and of the courage and principles it requires. Students can grapple with such questions as, What events today, in your own lives, require this sort of courage? These principles? Why was an institution as cruel as slavery so acceptable to so many citizens in the United States? What economic and social conditions supported it? What is the chance that slavery again could become acceptable in the United States?

The third solution raises the question, How do we know when students are engaged? They are engaged when they "devote substantial time and effort to a task, when they care about the quality of their work, and when they commit themselves, because the work seems to have significance beyond its personal, instrumental value" (Newmann 1986). Being engaged is thus more than being excited, for it involves being *challenged*.

Trends in Social Studies Education

Some of the trends now appearing in social studies concern content selection, global education, increased requirements, and a narrower focus.

Trend #1: Back to Curriculum

Because student disengagement in social studies is a persistent problem, social studies educators through the '70s and '80s focused a great deal of attention on improving instruction. Cooperative learning, discussion, guided practice, simulations, and the infusion of higher-order thinking have been recommended time and time again. Nevertheless, the familiar rote-oriented recitation method is still dominant. While frustration with this predicament can focus yet more attention on instructional variables, the trend for the 1990s is to consider also the curriculum side of the coin. *Good instruction on unimportant content is no victory.* Social studies educators are asking anew: What social studies knowledge is most important, and how can opportunities to learn it sensibly be sequenced across the grades, K-12?

Trend #2: Strengthening Content

One effect of the first trend is another: the increasing demand for history, geography, and civics in all grades. All of the curriculum proposals reviewed in this chapter concentrate on these three subjects. Economics is given some attention, too; the behavioral sciences (sociology, anthropology, and psychology) are barely mentioned. I am unaware of educators who claim the behavioral sciences are not important. Rather, the thinking seems to be that in the pre-collegiate years, foundations must be laid; the center must hold. The school day is short, and the available learning time is even shorter. Given this scarcity, time must be spent on helping students build the most essential understandings. Just what are they? This clearly is *the* critical question, one that curriculum planning committees should discuss at length, seeking an array of advice. My advice is contained in the five themes given in Chapter l: the democratic ideal, cultural diversity, economic development, global perspective, and participatory citizenship. Put more broadly still, social studies instruction should concentrate on U.S. and world history (both integrated with geography), international studies, and discussion of vital, persisting issues of public life. Of course, even this content is weak and inaccurate if it is not pervaded with multiple cultural perspectives.

Trend #3: Globalizing the Curriculum

While the world becomes more crowded, more interdependent, and more volatile, and while the East-West conflict is joined by the North-South conflict, only one-third to one-half of high school graduates in the United States take a world history course. Need there be better evidence of the extent to which essential learnings have been lost to the "smorgasbord curriculum" over the last two decades?

Requiring two years in the secondary grades of world history and geography is the most basic move a school system can make in the direction of introducing its students to the world beyond the shopping mall. Note that the National Commission on Social Studies in the Schools (1989) recommends a three-year *combination* of U.S. and world history, with geography for grades 9, 10, and 11. The Bradley Commission also recommends a two-year sequence of world history, but in the 8th and 9th grades.

Another very basic form of globalizing the social studies curriculum is to include international comparisons at each grade, in virtually every unit. Our 3rd grade teacher had students compare their own community with a community elsewhere in the world; the 8th grade teacher planned a unit on the Civil War that had students compare and contrast America's Lincoln and Tubman with South Africa's Tutu and Mandela; and the 11th grade teacher had students compare the United States with emerging democracies in Europe and

Latin America. The point here is to help students construct both knowledge and a disposition. They need to build accurate understandings—understandings that are not narrow or ethnocentric but that take international and cross-cultural variations into account—and they need to assemble a genuinely global habit of mind that inclines learners to *seek* global comparisons and to *want* the facts about the whole planet, not just their little piece of it.

Trend #4: Every Day, Every Grade

Ambitious trends like these, along with the public's recent outcry over students' pitiful knowledge of history, geography, and civics fuel the fourth trend: School boards are increasing requirements and replacing unessential electives like "mountaineering" and "American Cowboys" with requirements for U.S. and world history and geography and sustained discussions of recurrent public issues. Social studies textbook publishers are focusing on helping students build knowledge of ethnic diversity in the United States and elsewhere, even in the primary grades. Educators who specialize in teaching reading and writing skills are realizing that students can't read and write about nothing, and the logical subjects are social studies, science, and the arts and humanities. All of this adds up to a trend to provide daily instruction in social studies, K-12.

Trend #5: More on Less

The move to identify essential, foundational learnings in social studies and then to help students explore them in depth is associated with the last trend. Because it is the subject of Chapter 6, let me just note it here: It is the trend to spend precious instructional time on a limited number of important topics.

* * *

Social studies is by nature a controversial field. Reasonable people will disagree on a great many issues. Yet there is a national social studies curriculum—at least a national *written* curriculum. When teachers close the classroom door, however, they produce myriad taught curriculums in social studies. Some, especially in the primary grades, include no social studies at all. Choosing important knowledge, sequencing it well, and getting it behind every classroom door in every grade will be the curriculum committee's primary challenge.

References

Barber, B.R. (October 1989). "Public Talk and Civic Action." *Social Education* 53, 6: 355-356, 370.

Bradley Commission on History in the Schools. (1988). *Building a History Curriculum: Guidelines for Teaching History in Schools*. Washington, D.C.: Educational Excellence Network.

California State Board of Education. (1988). *History-Social Science Framework*. Sacramento, Calif.: California State Department of Education.

Dewey, J. (1915). *The Child and the Curriculum*. University of Chicago Press.

Evans, R. (September/October 1989). *Social Studies* 80, 5: special section.

Kniep, W.M. (October 1989). "Social Studies Within a Global Education." *Social Education* 53, 6: 399-403.

Morrissett, I., ed. (1982). *Social Studies in the 1980s: A Report of Project SPAN*. Alexandria, Va.: Association for Supervision and Curriculum Development.

National Commission on Social Studies in the Schools. (1989). *Charting A Course: Social Studies for the 21st Century*. Washington, D.C.

National Council for the Social Studies. (April 1979). "Revision of the NCSS Social Studies Curriculum Guidelines." *Social Education* 43, 261-78.

National Council for the Social Studies. (October 1989). "Report of the Ad Hoc Committee on Scope and Sequence." *Social Education* 53, 6: 375-376.

National Issues Forum in the Classroom (1990-91). National Issues Forum, 100 Commons Road, Dayton, OH, 45459.

Newmann, F.M. (April/May 1986). "Priorities for the Future." *Social Education* 50, 4: 240-250.

Newmann, F.M. (1988). "Higher Order Thinking in High School Social Studies: An Analysis of Classrooms, Teachers, Students and Leadership." Unpublished manuscript. National Center on Effective Secondary Schools. Madison: University of Wisconsin.

Newmann, F.M., T.A. Bertocci, and R.M. Landsness. (1977). *Skills in Citizen Action*. Madison: University of Wisconsin.

Noddings, N. (1984). *Caring*. Berkeley: University of California Press.

Parker, W.C. (in press). "Achieving Thinking and Decision-Making Objectives in Social Studies." In *Handbook of Research on Social Studies Teaching and Learning*, edited by James P. Shaver. New York: Macmillan.

Ravitch, D. (Summer 1987). "Tot Sociology." *American Scholar* 56, 3: 343-354.

Reimer, J., D.P. Paolitto, and R.H. Hersh. (1983). *Promoting Moral Growth* (2nd ed.). New York: Longman.

Shaughnessy, J.M., and T.M. Haladyna. (November/December 1985). "Research on Student Attitude Toward Social Studies." *Social Education* 49, 8: 692-695.

Shaver, J.P., O.L. Davis, and S.W. Helburn. (1979). *An Interpretative Report on the Status of Pre-collegiate Social Studies Education Based on Three NSF-Funded Studies*. Washington, D.C.: National Science Foundation.

Slavin, R.E. (1986). *Using Student Team Learning* 3rd ed. Baltimore, Md.: Johns Hopkins University.

Superka, D.P., P.L. Johnson, and C. Ahrens. (1975). *Values Education: Approaches and Materials*. Boulder, Colo.: ERIC Clearinghouse for Social Studies/Social Science Education Consortium.

Task Force on Scope and Sequence. (October 1989). "In Search of a Scope and Sequence for Social Studies." *Social Education* 53, 6: 376-385.

The World Around Us. (1990). New York: Macmillan Publishing Co.

Woyach, R.B., and R.C. Remy. (1989). *Approaches to World Studies: A Handbook for Curriculum Planners*. Boston, Mass.: Allyn & Bacon.

6
Thoughtful Learning and Authentic Assessment

This morning I was walking out, and I got over the fence. I saw the wheat a-holding up its head, looking very big. I went up and I took hold of it. You believe it—there was no wheat there! I said, 'God, what is the matter with this wheat?' And He said to me, 'Sojourner, there is a little weevil in it.'

Now I hear talking about the Constitution and the rights of man. I come up and I take hold of this Constitution. It looks mighty big, but when I feel for my rights, there ain't any there. Then I say, 'God, what ails this Constitution?'

He says to me, 'Sojourner, there is a little weevil in it!'

—Sojourner Truth

SOJOURNER WAS IN HER 50S, A FREED SLAVE, WHEN SHE SPOKE THESE WORDS to Ohio farmers in the years just before the Civil War. The weevil analogy was clear in that part of the country where crops had been devastated. The weevil in the Constitution, of course, was slavery. It had already consumed countless lives and was now eating clean through the new union.

There is a weevil in the public school system as well. It undermines the school's potential as a place of learning, especially in the secondary grades, and it undermines the best efforts of curriculum planners. It is this: Students are not held accountable in authentic ways for their schoolwork. Put differently, students are not challenged to show their best on benchmark tasks that are important, sensible, and worth striving for.

Of course, there is much testing and grading going on; these are, after all, conventions of school life. Like the wheat viewed from a distance, this activity looks very big. When you get up close, however, and try to take hold of it, you see there is *nothing* there. Students receive their diplomas without having to submit in exchange anything (not even *one* thing) of genuine value! Granted, they submit a transcript of credits earned, but transcripts indicate only that particular courses have been "taken," whatever *that* means. The point is that it doesn't mean much. The transcript reveals nothing of the content of the courses and nothing of what was actually learned, or to what degree. Transcripts permit no inferences regarding understandings built, abilities honed, or habits formed. The high school diploma is thus summarily stripped of meaning. No one can take seriously the notion of *earning* a diploma; students just get one if they go through the paces.

Yet the diploma is not stripped of its use, which explains its resilience. It still functions as a sort of visa. Without it, college and job entrance can be impeded. Devoid of authentic meaning, the diploma still serves bureaucratic purposes, and with a little work, we can make it serve learning purposes, too.

This chapter proposes the work that is needed. The first section gives the meaning of authentic assessment; the latter sketches the sort of curriculum and instruction with which such assessment should be combined.

Authentic Assessment

Teach to the test? The mere suggestion curdles the serious educator's blood. For many of us it brings to mind those awful standardized tests to which teachers presently are asked to teach, particularly the commercially available tests that are used to compare students' mathematics and reading scores across schools and districts and to which elementary teachers (and politicians, superintendents, and media) devote so much time.

The problem with these tests is that while they may be standardized, they are not *standard-setting* (Wiggins 1989). Thus, they are not *worth* teaching to or, for that matter, learning to, and certainly they should not serve as models of assessment for the social studies field. These tests are so bleak, so removed from real-life problems and expectations, so peripheral to the important learnings the diploma ought to reward—in a word, so unauthentic—that they have given a bad name to the idea of teaching to tests.

Actually, teaching to tests is precisely what we in social studies need to begin to do. But the tests will have to become the sorts of tests that set standards to which we are proud to teach and learn. Preparing for these tests should enrich learning, not reduce it. What sorts of tests are these? Consider the attributes listed in Figure 6.1.

FIGURE 6.1

Attributes of Authentic Benchmark Assessments

1. Tasks go to the heart of essential learnings, i.e., they ask for exhibitions of understandings and abilities that matter.
2. Tasks resemble interdisciplinary real-life challenges, not schoolish busywork that is artificially neat, fragmented, and easy to grade.
3. Tasks are standard-setting; they point students toward higher, richer levels of knowing.
4. Tasks are worth striving toward and practicing for.
5. Tasks are known to students well in advance.
6. Tasks are few in number; hence, they are representative.
7. Tasks strike teachers as worth the trouble.
8. Tasks generally involve a higher-order challenge—a challenge for which students have to go beyond the routine use of previously learned information.
9. All tasks are attempted by all students.

These attributes add up to more than a better test. They add up to an "exhibition of mastery" (Wiggins 1989)—a performance of important understandings and abilities. This decidedly *intellectual* performance is comparable to recitals in music, plays in theater, debates in law, and tournaments or games in athletics. None of these are perfunctory, bureaucratic checkups conducted to collect marks in a gradebook. Rather, they meet the requirements of authenticity—of functional (real-life) learning and ecological validity:

> Just as instruction should focus on learning to achieve genuine objectives, so too should assessment be anchored in tasks that have

genuine purposes. . . . Authenticity of assessment (thus) has strong
implications for the assessment-learning relationship (Valencia et
al. 1990).

Three implications are paramount. First, an assessment activity
must look and feel like a learning activity; that is, we should not ask
students to do on an assessment task something that we would not
ask them to do as part of a regular classroom learning activity.
Second, assessment tasks should involve higher-order challenge
rather than require only the regurgitation of information already
gathered; that is, students should be asked to do things for which the
routine use of previously learned information is not sufficient. Third,
assessment tasks should establish performance-based criteria for
learning that let students know, in a straightforward way, what it
means to do their schoolwork well. Together, these implications
show that authentic assessment can be a standard-setting tool for
improving curriculum and instruction as well as student learning.

While the first attribute in Figure 6.1 addresses the importance of
the learnings assessed, the others suggest the logic of authentic
assessment. The tasks reveal to students and parents what the
schoolwork is aiming toward, the sort of performance a student
should be striving for. Because the items are not kept secret, students
can mobilize their own resources—their initiative, study skills, and
perseverance, for example—in pursuit of these high standards. The
dutiful amassing of credits and courses is no longer the goal; courses
become opportunities, some better than others, to develop and hone
the understandings and abilities needed to perform well at the
exhibition.

In Chapter 2, I present several examples of social studies
learnings that could be demonstrated at the end of elementary,
middle, and high school. I call these benchmark assessments, as they
occur when a student is about to partake in an academic rite of
passage. The most important of these, the point at which our time
and energy will be most profitably spent, at least in the initial stages
of implementing authentic assessment, is the passage from high
school, signaled by the diploma. After this culminating assessment
has been planned, piloted, and revised, attention can turn to the
middle and elementary school assessments.

Let me suggest six learnings that get to the heart of what's
essential in social studies and might, therefore, be gathered into a
senior portfolio that students submit along with their request for a

diploma. Responses to these items are written, thus doubling as authentic samples of student writing ability.

Geography/International Studies. Three prominent international conflicts are drawn from the newspaper during the month the exhibition is scheduled. The student selects one of the three, writes a summary of the conflict, and discusses the influence of climate, resources, and location on the conflict. As well, the student sketches from memory a map of that region of the world showing national boundaries, capitals, and salient landforms. A legend and compass rose are included.

Ethnic Diversity. The student describes the changing ethnic diversity and relations among ethnic groups of North America from the 12th century to today and forecasts ethnic composition 25 years hence.

Civics/History. Three prominent national/local public issues are drawn from the newspaper during the month of the exhibition. The student selects one and summarizes all sides, takes a position, and argues for the position using at least one historical parallel.

Civics/History. The student identifies, then compares and contrasts, a diverse set of examples of societies organized under, or attempting to organize under, the democratic ideal. Examples should be drawn from three continents.

Citizenship. The student analyzes a transcribed excerpt of a discussion of a recurring public issue, distinguishing among factual, definitional, and ethical issues, and judging the quality of each participant's contribution.

Citizenship. The student correctly answers 90 percent of the questions on the citizenship test given by federal judges to immigrants seeking U.S. citizenship.

Note that only the last item lacks higher-order challenge. Although it does not require students to go beyond previously learned information, it is authentic on all other counts, and it has received immediate favorable response from audiences of parents and teachers. Most of us have admired the non-English speaking immigrants who successfully answer questions about the Constitution and Bill of Rights, Congress, and U.S. history. It is absurd that our high school graduates receive diplomas without having demonstrated the same.

The other items require a display not only of social studies knowledge but of higher-order thinking. The first and third items require students to analyze and to compose a summary on the spot. The third requires students to pull from memory a piece of history that informs the issue at hand. The second item has students forecast the future based on current information. The fourth has students compare and contrast the attributes of democracy as they appear under diverse conditions. The fifth requires analysis and judgment.

Of course, scoring criteria will have to be worked out. This is an important, but secondary problem. The primary problem is identifying the kinds of exhibitions. We can worry later about "a fair, efficient, and objective method for grading them" (Wiggins 1989). I have seen too many discussions of authentic assessment get bogged down by arguments about scoring.

Why don't we continue plugging away at improving instruction in social studies rather than trying to implement a new form of assessment? The main reason is that without authentic assessment, there are no straightforward, high standards to guide instruction *or* learning. Clearly, school district curriculum objectives do not serve this purpose. They may point to subject areas in which instruction should be planned, but they point to no standards, and they hold no one accountable.

My point is that both authentic assessment and improved instruction are critical components of a good education and a meaningful diploma. One cannot be developed without the other. Indeed, authentic assessment encourages improved instruction. The high standards for learning contained in the assessment—analyzing and summarizing public controversies; having the world map in mind; knowing history well enough to inform one's judgment on contemporary problems; and forecasting—these become standards for instruction as well. Imagine students trying to draw a historical parallel to support their position on a public controversy without having been taught what a historical parallel is or having examined rich historical material from which parallels might be drawn or having been given sustained opportunities, with feedback, to draw them carefully. Also, imagine students trying to summarize all sides of a public controversy without having been asked regularly in their classes to look at more than one side of an issue, or to take positions and defend them by clarifying and exploring all sides.

Curriculum and Instruction

Engaging Lessons

I recently sat with a group of high school history and government teachers who were attending an afternoon inservice program on teaching thinking skills in the content areas. The presenter was exhorting her audience to select and define several thinking skills (e.g., predicting, evaluating information, classifying) and "infuse them into your content areas so that your lessons teach content and thinking at the same time."

When it came time to work together at the department tables, the social studies teachers quickly completed the assignment so they would have something to share later during group reports. They chose predicting and outlined a lesson that any of them could use "in an emergency" or on a "substitute day." This obligation out of the way, an interesting conversation ensued during the remaining group time. They argued that social studies lessons should not have to be engaging. Rather, students should so desperately need to learn social studies content that their teachers could get away with unengaging instruction. Japan was given as an example of a nation where students are so driven to get the information needed to do well on the standardized exams that they make do with notoriously poor instruction. One of the teachers, who taught an Advanced Placement history course, testified to the power of that standardized exam to motivate student learning. He as much as admitted that his instruction could be quite mediocre since his students were so motivated.

At the conclusion of the thinking skills program, the social studies group asked their principal to schedule a meeting to investigate a testing program in social studies. They hoped their students might thus be encouraged to pay more attention to their studies—"to take their medicine."

This argument is intriguing. On the one hand, the group was recognizing, quite rightly, the untapped potential of benchmark examinations to motivate students to pay attention during class, complete homework, and study. On the other hand, the group was rationalizing poor instruction, arguing that students should not *need* good instruction. Here is the point: The sort of assessment these teachers were imagining was not authentic; it was the standardized, not standard-setting, sort for which no alteration in their curriculum and instruction would be required. Granted, the implementation of benchmark standardized exams would probably motivate students to "take their medicine." But so what? Aside from making the job of an unambitious instructor easier, the cause of meaningful learning is not advanced, students' schoolwork is not pointed toward high standards, and a public trust is violated: Professional educators are employed by the public to organize subject matter and provide instruction in ways that an amateur could not. Meaningful learning, high standards, and trust—these are the stakes.

Depth of Content

This social studies department notwithstanding, social studies educators are generally sympathetic to the argument that good instruction is needed. This has been their tradition at least since the progressive era, when reaction tc the recitation/rote memory model began in earnest (Hertzberg 1989). But their interest in good instruction is often coupled with two blindspots. We just discussed one of these, the failure to conduct authentic assessments. The other concerns the opposite side of the curriculum and instruction coin: curriculum.

Amid the eagerness to improve instruction, too little attention has been paid to deciding which subject matter the improved instruction should help students achieve. This is folly. The best teaching methods cannot possibly overcome a weak curriculum; good instruction on unimportant content is no victory. All the hullabaloo over discovery learning (Taba 1963), reciprocal learning (Palinscar and Brown 1984), direct instruction (Hunter 1982), cooperative learning (Johnson and Johnson 1988), and learning styles (Dunn, Beaudry, and Klavas 1989) is wasted when the particular learnings to which they are directed are unimportant. Conversely, their missions are fulfilled when the learnings are essential.

In-depth study provides leverage on this problem by bringing improved instruction and curriculum into consideration simultaneously. In-depth study means that more instructional time is spent on fewer topics *and* that the additional time is used to lead students "beyond superficial exposure to rich, complex understanding" (Newmann 1988a). Hence the slogan, "more on less."

More on less has to be contrasted with less on more. *Covering* material is a well-known euphemism in social studies for providing a little instruction on many topics. This is superficial instruction, best characterized as teaching by mentioning. When the so-called cultural literacy lobby (Hirsch 1987) produces its lists of what everybody should know, the items they recommend become new candidates for a mention somewhere in the curriculum. When state legislatures mandate still more student learning objectives (e.g., AIDS and drugs education) these topics, too, get mentioned. Whole courses, like U.S. history or world history, may degenerate to parades of mentioned people, places, events, and dates.

Consider the student's point of view on superficial coverage. John, a student in a better-than-average high school, was asked to describe a time he had been given the opportunity to study a topic for at least two weeks. He remembered only one such opportunity.

> I got totally immersed in a project when the teacher forced us to do a paper on some guy. We couldn't pick him, but we had to read at least four books and write at least 100 note cards—big cards—and develop at least a ten-page paper. I got Montaigne. It ended up real interesting. As Mr. Foster pointed out, it was kind of cool that I got to be a real expert and to know more than probably five million people in America about this guy. I'm not sure what made it so interesting—whether it was Montaigne's own works and life or just the fact that I got to know so much about him (Newmann 1988b).

John added that he had not been given many of these opportunities. Much of the time, he said,

> It's a total skim; it's very bad. The course in European history is a classic example. We covered 2,000 years. Every week we were assigned to cover a 30-page chapter. The teacher is a stickler for dates and facts. We had 50 dates a week to memorize. The pity of it all is that now I don't remember any of them. I worked so hard, and now basically all I remember is Montaigne. There's like maybe five dates I remember, when I probably learned 300 or 400 dates all year. I can't even remember a lot of the major guys we studied.

The "total skim" approach may have cost John the opportunity to develop a rich network of understandings about history, geography, and government—understandings that might initially have been developed in the elementary grades, then extended and refined in the secondary grades. The countless tests taken, questions answered, worksheets completed, and hours of attention to teachers' and textbooks' expositions did not bear fruit enough for John: "I worked so hard, and now basically all I remember is Montaigne."

In-depth study is worth time and trouble because it promises so much that social studies educators value: rich understandings, better transfer, thoughtfulness, and a powerful support for curriculum renewal efforts. We will look briefly at each.

Rich Understandings. Probably no one argues that superficial exposure to a great number of topics helps students develop rich understandings. Instead, we hear that superficial exposure is necessitated by the teacher's own breadth of knowledge. "What am I supposed to do," one high school teacher asked me, "skip over the Industrial Revolution altogether? Or, better that I skip the Civil War? The World Wars? The Vietnam War?" For this teacher, it would be intellectually dishonest not to at least mention these topics. But, as another teacher commented, it is this breadth of personal knowledge that a good teacher tries to manage carefully: "The more a teacher knows, the more important it is that the teacher have an effective pedagogy to hold the information in restraint" (Onosko 1989).

Superficial coverage is also necessitated by external factors such as school district curriculum guidelines or the impending AP course exam. One teacher testifies (Onosko 1989, p. 186):

> There is a comprehensive exam given the second week in May covering all the material from the 1600s to the present. This puts tremendous pressure on my classes to move through the material quickly.

This same teacher said she would side with coverage over depth even if the AP exam did not push her to do so. Even if the external pressure was removed, the internal pressure remains:

> If I had to make a choice I would choose coverage because . . . I really feel an obligation to at least expose them to some of the pressing issues of our time. Not to get to the 1950s and 1960s, the Cold War . . . is unconscionable . . . . I think it is more important that they get exposure and that means sacrificing depth . . . . I want to give them as much exposure as I can, you know, shove it down their throats.

None of these teachers is arguing that superficial exposure is an attempt to help students understand the material at hand, or that it results in anything more than a vague familiarity with the material. No, superficial exposure, when defended, is considered the lesser of two evils: Skipping material would be "unconscionable." Should we, then, give up this goal? Renewing the social studies curriculum

RENEWING THE SOCIAL STUDIES CURRICULUM

requires not only that we keep this goal but that we begin to take it seriously. First, however, we have to examine it.

Building understandings is distinct from warehousing information and skills. This is still true when the information is historical information and the skills are the now-popular thinking skills. As distinct from warehousing, understanding should be appreciated as the distinct human achievement it is. An understanding is constructed in the mind of the learner. It is an interpretation or model of a situation that the learner is working to comprehend. An understanding is assembled and built up, like a castle, not "discovered," like oil or gold (Novak and Gowin 1984, Vosniadou and Brewer 1987).

As a human construction, an understanding results from the constructive efforts of the learners themselves, working under the guidance of a teacher. The teacher knows what sorts of efforts her students should engage in so as to produce their understandings, and this is precisely the work she has them do. To be sure, this work includes mastery of many details, but it involves much more than data gathering, and it surely does not require that the data gathering be completed before the other, higher- order work begins. (The common insistence that students have the "background" information *before* they begin their higher-order explorations is uninformed.)

What is this other, higher-order work? A compendium of intellectual labor: comparing and contrasting examples, seeking out exceptions to rules, posing questions and hypotheses, analyzing the values that fuel controversies, exploring and clarifying perspectives that are different from one's own, adding relief to the terrain with rich historical literature, interrogating one's conclusions, and so on. The model is revised as one goes along.

Understanding is thus inconceivable with only superficial exposure to a topic, and this is what is so disappointing about the new California social studies framework (1988): It flies in the face of what we now know about the construction of understandings in the student's mind. By "thirding" U.S. history, as I note at the end of Chapter 3, the California framework obstructs the intellectual labor needed if students are to build up any real, substantive understandings of U.S. history. The needed constructive work requires a pedagogy of *layering*—helping students form an initial understanding of a topic, then returning to the same topic later to build a deeper understanding, and returning again for a still deeper understanding. For example, students can form an initial, vague sense of democracy in the 5th grade, returning to democracy in the 8th grade, only now correcting misconceptions (including the classic misunderstanding that democracy means, simply, majority rule) and adding another, deeper, richer layer of meaning. At the 8th grade, this might be accomplished through biographical studies of key democrats. The curriculum can return students to democracy again in the high school U.S. history course, now delving into what seriously can be considered an advanced level of understanding: grappling with the public issues that citizens in democracies must confront, such as the conflicts between freedom and authority, individual liberty and the public good, and the like. It is bizarre that the California framework slices U.S. history into bits, with years in between, in the name of in-depth study. In effect, because only the first layer of each bit is studied, the opposite of in-depth understanding is predictably achieved: superficial knowledge filled inevitably with much misconception.

Transfer. Understanding is not all that is sacrificed to superficial coverage. Transfer, too, is made less likely. A basic goal of schooling is that knowledge and skills achieved in one subject be applied to others and used in everyday life. For example, if students have studied in some depth the Russian and French revolutions in their 10th grade world history class, we want them to use that knowledge in the 11th grade to elaborate their understanding of the English colonists' revolt in North America. Indeed, the U.S. history teacher's unit plan should prompt this transfer. Comparing and contrasting the three upheavals, students can then begin to assemble a general, transferable understanding of popular revolts that can be used elsewhere, including examinations of present conditions in China, South Africa, or Rumania.

Fortunately, much can be done to promote transfer, but little of it can be done in a "total skim" instructional environment. Students who have stored in short-term memory a few facts about the Russian and French revolutions and the colonists' War for Independence will not know enough about either to break them down into issues, problems, events, actors, arguments, and other properties. Consequently, it will be nearly impossible to compare and contrast them, let alone to draw parallels with conflicts in the world today (Spiro et al. 1987).

Thoughtfulness. In addition to putting understanding and transfer at risk, superficial coverage undermines the disposition we want most to cultivate in social studies: thoughtfulness (Schrag 1988, see also Cornbleth 1985). By thoughtfulness I mean those habits of mind that incline one to behave reflectively—to *think*, to construct a model of the situation when impulsiveness or avoidance are tempting. Think of Socrates' habits: the open and unashamed admission of ignorance, the consideration of all sides of the case. Like other virtues, these are honed over years of expectation (others expect you to form them), examination (you grapple with them and monitor their development), and coaxing (significant others care that you form these habits and hold you accountable).

Contrast this with the habits of thought*lessness* honed in the total skim environment: Knowledge is the acquisition of a few facts on a given topic, especially names, whether of people (Washington, Lenin, Lincoln), places (Egypt, Nebraska), or ideas (democracy, continent, civilization). If one knows the names, one is not ignorant. Learning is the warehousing of these names. Hilda Taba called this superficial, name-deep knowledge the "rattle of empty wagons" (see Parker and Perez 1987).

While a thoughtful disposition cannot replace intellectual skills, we must acknowledge that the skills are of little value without the disposition. Research indicates that instruction on skill use can be quite effective, but that the skill very well may not be used after the instruction ends. Post- instructional use of skills depends largely on learners' developing the disposition to use the skills they have learned (Belmont et al. 1982).

The Key Question. Finally, in-depth study is a boost to curriculum renewal. This is because it pushes into consideration the question, What topics deserve in-depth study? Without the need to reduce the number of topics covered, planners might never have to grapple seriously with this question.

Thoughtful Classrooms

In-depth study means spending more instructional time on fewer topics, and using the additional time to help students construct rich, complex understandings. Several examples of the needed "construction work" were given above, including comparing and contrasting examples and interrogating conclusions.

Educators have gone to great lengths to spell out the kinds of intellectual labor a student might need to undertake (Marzano et al.

1988). This work led to the thinking skills movement. While developing students' thinking skills is an important endeavor, even thinking skills can be "covered" superficially, and once "covered" they may never be applied to the construction of the understandings we desperately want our students to have. Thinking skills instruction does not get to the heart of the problem.

It will be more helpful if we point our efforts toward creating thoughtful classrooms. This is the basic work, for it occurs at the most fundamental level: the classroom social setting.

To create more thoughtful classrooms, we need to understand what they are and how they differ from less thoughtful classrooms. In-depth study is one (perhaps *the*) critical attribute of thoughtful classrooms. But there are others. Newmann (1988b) has clarified six dimensions of thoughtful classrooms.

1. *A few topics are examined in depth rather than many topics covered superficially.*

2. *Lessons have substantive coherence and continuity.* In thoughtful classrooms, unrelated bits of information are pulled together.

3. *Students are given time to think—to prepare responses to questions.* Students in thoughtful classrooms, whether responding orally or in writing, have time to think, time to initiate as well as to respond, time to reflect, and time to produce more elaborate responses.

4. *The teacher asks challenging questions and structures challenging tasks.* By definition, thinking is unnecessary when routine application of already learned information will suffice. Consequently, the construction and elaboration of historical (and other) understandings requires challenges that involve novel, nonroutine work.

5. *The teacher is a model of thoughtfulness.* This key disposition—thoughtfulness—is expressed through the teacher's interaction with students and the topic at hand. For example, the teacher reveals her own grappling with difficult points, shows students how she thought through a challenge, and appreciates their mental work and alternative approaches to problems.

6. *Students offer explanations and reasons for their conclusions.* In thoughtful classrooms, students are accustomed to supporting their answers and conclusions by producing reasons and explanations.

This list of elements of thoughtful classrooms is broadly useful. The six indicators should be observed across a variety of teaching styles (the counselor, the warm demander) and classroom organizations (cooperative teams, large groups). The indicators should be observed in the teaching of an array of topics at virtually any grade. They should be observed, too, in the teaching of a variety of skills, from discussion skills to thinking skills. Perhaps most important, they should be used by teachers who want to refine their own teaching and become more adept planners of higher-order challenges.

A Thoughtful Curriculum

We have seen that social studies lessons and classrooms can be thoughtful, but can a whole K-12 curriculum? I think it can. Like the thoughtful classroom, the thoughtful curriculum has its own necessary attributes. In this case, the emphasis is less on student-teacher interactions and more on the way that all the pieces fit together across the grades.

Before listing the attributes, let me recall the problems that make a thoughtful curriculum elusive. Overall, there are four. The first concerns the school's mission: If learning were truly the mission, we would see much more discussion and debate among faculty and building leaders about content selection and engaging lessons. The key question is, Learn *what*? We must leave behind broad, blanket answers like "social studies," or "U.S. history and geography." We have to become more specific.

The second problem area concerns the lack of grade-to-grade curriculum coherence, or articulation. When 5th grade teachers plan their U.S. history curriculum, they need to know that their students were introduced to the regional geography of North America and the history of their state in 4th grade. Likewise, 10th grade world history teachers need to know that their students have already studied world cultural geography and have the world map well in mind. In the absence of this grade-to-grade coherence, the social studies curriculum is needlessly splintered and needlessly repetitive *at the beginning levels of understanding*. Teachers feel they have to start at the lowest rung on the ladder, and the construction of more sophisticated understandings is undermined. Many ideas are introduced but few are elaborated and deepened.

Third, personnel selection and retention procedures are remarkably weak and sometimes scandalous. If the first two problem areas are to be addressed—if the social studies curriculum is to be renewed—then people with strong subject matter knowledge are needed to fill the ranks of both faculty and administration. Poor teachers and poor administrators alike are going to have to be removed.

Fourth, the diploma has lost its meaning as a measure of learning. This problem alone permits the first three to continue unabated. Authentic assessment procedures should be devised and piloted without delay.

In the elementary grades, these problems appear in myriad forms, the most unfortunate of which is the lack of articulation between the reading curriculum—the centerpiece of the elementary school—and essential learnings in history, geography, and civics. In the secondary grades, the subjugation of the learning mission to athletics—the centerpiece of many high schools—is perhaps the most pervasive threat to a thoughtful curriculum, infecting both personnel selection and the culture of the school. But running close behind are the lack of articulation across courses, the separation of history from the arts for all but the high track, the loss of world history to electives, and the remarkable ease with which a student who has developed no understanding of democracy or ethnic diversity can pass through the grades and receive a diploma. As a college student told me, "I couldn't *spell* diploma and they gave me one."

Attributes of the Thoughtful Curriculum

The first attribute is the deliberate selection of essential subject matter that virtually all students study. If tracking denies equal access to important learnings, the curriculum cannot be called a thoughtful one.

Second, a thoughtful curriculum promotes the incremental development and elaboration of understandings across grade levels. Practically, this means that essential subject-matter strands are spiraled though the K-12 curriculum, and a sequence of learning opportunities is planned so that strand-related understandings are constructed systematically. Democracy, for example is revisited several times so that misconceptions can be corrected and the understanding made more elaborate and precise. Strands should not be so broad (e.g., history, economics, change) that they provide no guidance for content selection when teachers are planning units.

Third, a thoughtful social studies curriculum has a civic mission, which is the preparation of citizens for popular sovereignty. Teachers at all grade levels should have clearly in mind, and be able to discuss with students, the relationship of their social studies lessons to this mission. Reference to benchmark assessments, which make the relationship clear, should help.

Fourth, content is selected and organized to make student engagement likely. While engagement is more an attribute of a thoughtful social studies lesson or classroom than of a K-12 curriculum, it can be facilitated by the design of the curriculum. For example, a limited number of objectives are written for each grade level or course in order to encourage in-depth study; discussions of contemporary and historical public controversies are built systematically into the K-12 scope and sequence; multiple examples of key topics (e.g., slavery, democracy) are selected for examination to encourage in-depth study and higher-order comparisons; and international comparisons are planned to elaborate what otherwise would be a thin, provincial understanding.

Fifth, only faculty with considerable knowledge of the subject are assigned to teach it. Once assigned, their knowledge base is strengthened through subject-specific staff development programs, for example, teaching public issues in the middle school history class.

Sixth, a thoughtful curriculum is guided by, and pointed toward, preparing students for authentic exhibitions of their learning.

Finally, a thoughtful social studies curriculum is supervised by someone knowledgeable of the attributes of such a curriculum.

An Example

Let's consider an example of just one piece of a thoughtful social studies curriculum, focusing on only a few grades and just two of the five strands: democracy and participatory citizenship.

It is generally useful to plan these strands together so that they provide both an intellectual and experiential perspective on the democratic ideal. This ideal is the tradition of increasing liberty and rising hope. In the lower grades, children can be introduced to the democratic ideal by studying people who, like Washington, Madison, and Paul Revere, fought for democracy in the United States, as well as those who, like Lincoln, Sojourner Truth, King, and so many others, struggled to improve it. Textbooks used in combination with children's literature and oral histories make this feasible.

Meanwhile, the children can enrich their democratic study with democratic experiences. The approach I favor is regular democratic *practice*: participation in democratic classroom meetings (Shaheen 1989). Here, children learn firsthand about majority rule and minority rights, about due process, and about the central work in a democracy, deliberation. Whether the issues are playground troubles or welcoming new children to the classroom, they are public issues nonetheless and require discussion and the formulation of policy.

In the 5th grade, the meetings should continue while students concentrate on a chronological history of democracy in the United States. As well, the history and geography of North America prior to the European influx should be studied in depth. Krensky's (1987) *Who Really Discovered America?* gives children a feel for the American land before humans appeared, and most 5th grade history textbooks provide information on the Iroquois League, which centuries later was to influence the U.S. Constitution (Weatherford 1988).

International comparisons on the democratic ideal should be included in the 8th grade history course. Now that students have a broad idea of the U.S. case, their understanding can be elaborated strategically to include a few other cases of democracy—Mexico, Canada, Costa Rica, the new Poland, and ancient Athens, for example. Using jigsaw-style cooperative teams, a handful of cases can be studied efficiently. Bridging the study of history with contemporary civic life, classroom meetings can be directed toward discussing policy controversies facing the local community. Looking ahead to the benchmark assessment scheduled at the end of middle/junior high school, students should be taught to use their historical understandings in the analysis of these contemporary problems. A law and justice course in the 9th grade can take on the analysis of local issues in earnest.

It is in the high school social studies curriculum that the attributes of a thoughtful curriculum are least often found. Here an observer is likely to find American history taught in isolation from American literature, no curriculum coordination and supervision, and sometimes scandalous personnel selection and retention practices. Yet, a curriculum committee can take steps to make renewal both exciting and feasible. The following is my favorite plan for topics to be studied during high school.

- **10th Grade**: *World History* with special attention to in-depth study of the ethnic diversity of selected civilizations and the conditions supporting democratic and totalitarian institutions.
- **11th Grade**: *U.S. History* with special attention to analyzing and discussing public policy controversies and drawing historical parallels. Teachers and students use the textbook for background information—the big picture—while digging into one or two

controversies that represent the spirit and problems of each era of U.S. history. Students explore the issues dialogically, that is, with a commitment to understanding all sides. Discussion skills are taught and practiced.

Excellent, low-cost materials are available. Perhaps the best is the *Public Issues Series* (1988), several slim booklets that supplement the U.S. history textbook. In the words of its authors, the series aims to:

> help students analyze and discuss persisting human dilemmas related to public issues . . . . Public issues is not synonymous with current events. By public issues, we mean problems or value dilemmas persisting throughout history and across cultures. The situations of Christian martyrs in Rome, a bureaucrat in Nazi Germany, a slave in 19th century America, or an Ethiopian refugee in Texas in 1988 represent important public issues . . . . All units in the series suggest parallels between historical illustrations of persisting human dilemmas and present issues in the United States and the world.

To date, six issue units are available: *American Revolution: Crisis of Law and Change; Immigration: Pluralism and National Identity; Organized Labor: Workers, Employers, and the Public Interest; The Civil War: Slavery and the Crisis of Union; The Progressive Era: The Limits of Reform;* and *The New Deal: Government and the Economy.*

• **12th Grade:** *Public Issues* is a one-semester course that extends and applies students' developing understanding of democracy and deliberation of public issues. Not the traditional how-a-bill- becomes-a-law course, Current Public Issues is dedicated to deliberation of contemporary public controversies. Thanks to New York's requirement that all 12th graders take such a course, several publishers have produced relevant materials. The best, in my view, is National Issues Forum in the Classroom (1990-91), a low-cost program that integrates in-depth study, field trips, and discussion.

* * *

The field of social studies education has a long road ahead before it can routinely produce thoughtful lessons, classrooms, and curriculums. Poor student accountability, low intellectual standards, superficial exposure, and unchallenging lessons unfortunately characterize social studies today. There are exceptions, but they are exceptions nonetheless. Yet the problems are workable. In this chapter, I presented a few promising building blocks—authentic assessment, in-depth study, higher-order challenge, and the systematic elaboration of understandings across grades and courses. With these as starting points, curriculum renewal in social studies can begin in earnest.

References

Belmont, J.M., E.C. Butterfield, and R.P. Ferretti. (1982). "To Secure Transfer of Training, Instruct Self-Management Skills." In *How and How Much Can Intelligence Be Increased?*, edited by D.K. Detterman and R.J. Sternberg. Norwood, N.J.: Ablex.

Cornbleth, C. (1985). "Critical Thinking and Cognitive Processes." *Review of Research in Social Studies Education: 1976-1983*, edited by W.B. Stanley. Washington, D.C.: National Council for the Social Studies.

Dunn. R., J. Beaudry, and A. Klavas. (March 1989). "Survey of Research on Learning Styles." *Educational Leadership* 46, 6: 50-58.

Hertzberg, H. (1989). "History and Progressivism: A Century of Reform Proposals." In *Historical Literacy*, edited by P. Gagnon. New York: Macmillan.

Hirsch, E.D., Jr. (1987). *Cultural Literacy*. New York: Houghton Mifflin.

Hunter, M. (1982). *Mastery Teaching*. El Segundo, Calif.: TIP Publications.

Immigration: Pluralism and National Identity. Teacher's Guide. (1989). Public Issues Series. Boulder, Colo.: Social Science Education Consortium.

Johnson, D.W., and R.T. Johnson. (May 1988). "Critical Thinking Through Structured Controversy." *Educational Leadership* 45, 8: 58-64.

Krensky, S. (1987). *Who Really Discovered America?* New York: Scholastic.

Marzano, R.J., R. Brandt, C.S. Hughes, B.F. Jones, B.Z. Presseisen, S.C. Rankin, and C. Suhor. (1988). *Dimensions of Thinking: A Framework for Curriculum and Instruction*. Alexandria, Va.: Association for Supervision and Curriculum Development.

National Issues Forum in the Classroom 1990-91. National Issues Forum, 100 Commons Road, Dayton OH, 45459.

Newmann. F.M. (1988a). "Can Depth Replace Coverage in the High School Curriculum?" *Phi Delta Kappan* 69, 5: 346.

Newmann, F.M. (1988b). "Higher-Order Thinking in High School Social Studies: An Analysis of Classrooms." (Report). National Center on Effective Secondary Schools. Madison: University of Wisconsin.

Novak, J.D. and D.B. Gowin (1984). *Learning How to Learn*. Cambridge: Cambridge University Press.

Onosko, J. (1989). "Comparing Teachers' Thinking About Promoting Students' Thinking." *Theory and Research in Social Education* 27, 3: 174-195.

Palinscar, A.S. and A.L. Brown. (1984). "Reciprocal Teaching of Comprehension Fostering and Monitoring Activities." *Cognition and Instruction* 1, 2: 117-175.

Parker, W.C.,and S.A. Perez. (March 1987). "Beyond the Rattle of Empty Wagons." *Social Education* 51, 3: 164-166.

Public Issues Series (1988). Social Science Education Consortium, 3300 Mitchell Lane #240, Boulder, CO 80301-2272.

Schrag, F. (1988). *Thinking in School and Society*. New York: Routledge.

Shaheen, J.C. (October 1989). "Participatory Citizenship in the Elementary Grades." *Social Education* 53, 6: 361-363.

Spiro, R.J., W.P. Vispoel, J. Schmitz, A. Samarapungavan, and A.E. Boerger. (1987). "Knowledge Acquisition for Application: Cognitive Flexibility and Transfer in Complex Content Domains." In *Executive Control Processes*, edited by B.C. Britton. Hillsdale, N.J.: Erlbaum.

Taba, H. (March 1963). "Learning by Discovery." *Elementary School Journal* 63, 6: 308-316.

Valencia, S., W. McGinley, and P.D. Pearson. (1990). "Assessing Reading and Writing: Building a More Complete Picture." In *Reading in the Middle School* (2nd ed.), edited by G. Duffy. Newark, Dele.: International Reading Association.

Vosniadou, S., and W.F. Brewer. (1987). "Theories of Knowledge Restructuring in Development." *Review of Educational Research* 57, 1: 51-67.

Weatherford, J. (1988). *Indian Givers: How the Indians of the Americas Transformed the World*. New York: Fawcett.

Wiggins, G. (April 1989). "Teaching to the Authentic Test." *Educational Leadership* 46, 7: 41-47.

Appendix 1

Social Studies and the Education of Citizens

Excerpted from "In Search of a Scope and Sequence for Social Studies," a report of the National Council for the Social Studies Task Force on Scope and Sequence. *Social Education* (October 1989): 376-387. Reprinted with permission.

Teachers and curriculum planners have to decide not only what goes into the social studies program but the order in which the components are to appear, i.e., their *sequence*. Presentation sequences should represent decisions based on the application of psychological principles of human development and of professional judgment. The Task Force does not recommend that a social studies sequence rely *solely* on the expanding-environment principle. The life space of today's children is greatly affected by modern methods of communication and transportation. Who should claim that the life space of a six-year-old is limited to the local environment when each evening the child may view television accounts of events *in progress* from anywhere in the world? Therefore, the social studies curriculum should not move sequentially from topics that are near-at-hand to those that are farther away for the purpose of expanding the environment. The purpose of extending content outward, away from a self-centric focus, is to illustrate how people and places interact; how people of different areas depend on one another; how people are part of interlocking networks that sustain the life of modern societies; and how people and places everywhere fit into a global human community. What young children see going on around them is being done in one way or another by human beings everywhere.

Complexity has been another commonly accepted rationale for arranging content in a particular sequence. Topics perceived as simple were placed earlier in the program than those thought to be more difficult. Experience has shown that it is probably not possible to develop a workable sequence based *solely* on the assumption of complexity of content. Topics *per se* are intrinsically neither simple nor complex. Their complexity is regulated by instructional variables: the concepts, relationships, and issues selected for study; the amount, quality and use of instructional materials; the pace of the presentation; the depth of understanding expected. This is illustrated by the fact that 1st graders and Ph.D. candidates in sociology both study the family, though at different levels of analysis. Scope-and-sequence charts that show subject matter arranged sequentially over a span of grades according to presumed difficulty may create erroneous impressions about the complexity of content.

The Task Force is recommending a *holistic-interactive* approach to the selection and placement of content. That is, content at *any* grade level should be presented in ways that provide, insofar as possible, a comprehensive view of a complex whole. Topics may be regarded as part of an interacting network that often extends worldwide. People everywhere arrange themselves in social groups and engage in basic social processes. The earth is the home of human beings no matter where they live individually. Potentially, all human beings can share in the legacies derived from all cultures. Subject matter at all grade levels needs to be taught from a global perspective. This approach is *interactive* because everything relates to everything else; it is *holistic* because it casts events in their broadest social context.

Illustrative Scope and Sequence—Content

The illustrative scope and sequence that follow deal with only one dimension of the social studies program—namely, the substantive content or subject matter. It is around this subject matter that skills and values (elaborated in other sections of this report) are taught. The material is presented for illustrative purposes and should not be construed as a model or ideal program. Rather, it is intended to extend the outer boundaries of existing practice, without moving so far out as to make the document unusable.

Grade Level Examples

Kindergarten—Awareness of Self in a Social Setting

The major thrust of the kindergarten program should be to provide socialization experiences that help children bridge their home life with the group life of the school. Teachers can expect considerable variation in the extent of kindergartners' experience in group settings. Some have been in day-care centers or preschools for two or more years. Others are entering a social environment that involves several other children for the first time. Learning about the physical and social environments of the school will thus be different for individual children. Nevertheless, they all need to begin to learn the reasons for rules as required for orderly social relationships. Awareness of self should be developed through face-to-face relationships with others in social settings. It is important at this level to provide children with success experiences to help them develop self-esteem. Some structured experiences to sensitize children to a world of many and diverse peoples and cultures need to be included.

Grade 1—The Individual in Primary Social Groups: Understanding School and Family Life

The socialization to school begun in kindergarten should be continued and extended in 1st grade. Basic concepts related to social studies content should be introduced. Children can learn the specialized roles of school personnel as an example of division of labor. Family life and structure, including variations of family structures, should be included, as well as roles of family members. Essential activities of a family in meeting basic material and psychological needs should be stressed. Variations in the way families live need to be studied: e.g., urban, rural, self-employed, single-parent family arrangements, and various housing options. Dependence of family members on one another and of the family on other families should be stressed. Children should learn that the family is the primary support group for people everywhere. The need for rules and laws should be taught as a natural extension of orderly group life. History can be presented through the study of the children's own families and the study of family life in earlier times. Learning about family life in other cultures provides opportunities for comparing ways of living. The globe should be introduced along with simple maps to promote learning of geographic concepts and relationships. It is important that the program include some study of the world beyond the neighborhood. Direct experience and hands-on activities are essential at this level, but the program should be organized around specific social studies goals and objectives rather than consisting of unstructured play activities in social settings.

Grade 2—Meeting Basic Needs in Nearby Social Groups: The Neighborhood

Meeting basic requirements of living in nearby social groups should be the central theme in 2nd grade. The program should emphasize that the neighborhood is the students' own unique place in space, and they should learn some of the ways their space interacts with the rest of the world. It is in the study of the neighborhood that students can and should learn on a firsthand basis some of the most elemental of human relationships such as sharing and caring, helping others in times of need, and living harmoniously with neighbors. The study of social functions such as education, production, consumption, communication, and transportation in a neighborhood context are appropriate as children develop an understanding and appreciation of people in groups. The need for rules and laws should be stressed and illustrated by examples from the everyday lives of children. Geographic concepts relating to direction and physical features of the landscape need to be included. A global perspective is important and can be sought through the study of neighborhood life in another culture. Contrasting neighborhood life today with what it was in an earlier time should also be included to provide historical perspective.

Grade 3—Sharing Earth Space with Others: The Community

The community in a global setting is the focus of study at the 3rd grade level. The local community provides an excellent laboratory for the study of social life because all aspects of social living take place there. But the concept of community should not be limited to the local area. It is essential that some attention be given to the global community. Social functions such as production, transportation, communication, distribution, and government, including their international connections, should be stressed. The concepts of dependence and interdependence can be emphasized at the local, national, and international levels. Geographic concepts and skills should be extended to include the interactions of human beings with the environment. Place location and map-reading skills must be stressed. Some emphasis should be given to the study of the history of the local community, especially relevant social history and biographies of prominent local citizens.

Grade 4—Human Life in Varied Environments: The Region

The 4th grade is the ideal level to focus on basic geographic concepts and related skills. The major emphasis in the 4th grade is the region, an area of the earth that is defined for a specific reason. Where state regulations require it, the home state may be studied as a political region. World geographic regions defined in terms of physical features, climate, agricultural production, industrial development, or economic level should be selected for study. Culture regions of the past and present may also be included. There should be some variation in the regions selected for study to illustrate the adaptability of human beings to varied environments. All the basic map- and globe-reading skills should be included in the program. History should be included in the units of study to show how places have changed over time. Economic concepts such as *resources, scarcity,* and *exchange* should be used to illustrate how regions of the world interact.

Grade 5—People of the Americas: The United States and Its Close Neighbors

The 5th grade program focuses on the development of the United States as a nation in the Western Hemisphere, with particular emphasis on developing affective attachments to those principles on which this nation was founded and that guided its development. The diverse cultural, ethnic, and racial origins of the American people should be stressed. Attention should be directed to specific individuals who have contributed to the political, social, economic, and cultural life of the nation. The inclusion of biographies of prominent American men and women of diverse ethnic origins is essential to highlight values embraced by this society. The 5th grade program should familiarize

learners with the history and geography of the closest neighbor nations of the
United States: Canada and Mexico.

Grade 6—People and Cultures: Representative World Regions

The focus of the 6th grade program is on selected people and cultures of
the Eastern Hemisphere and Latin America. The people and cultures should be
representative of (1) major geographical regions of the world; (2) levels of
economic development; (3) historical development; (4) political and value
systems. The interdependence of nations should be a major theme. Instruction
needs to be directed toward understanding and appreciating the lifeways of
other people through the development of such concepts as language, technology, institutions, and belief systems.

It is recommended that *at least* one semester of systematic study be devoted
to Latin America in either the 6th *or* 7th grade. The cultural, political, and
economic linkages with the United States should be emphasized. The growing
importance of Latin America in international political and economic affairs
should be stressed.

Grade 7—A Changing World of Many Nations: A Global View

The 7th grade program provides an opportunity to broaden the concept of
humanity within a global context. The focus should be on the world as the
home of many different people who strive to deal with the forces that shape
their lives. The search for—and the need for—peaceful relations among nations
needs to be stressed. The content is international in scope (including the
Western Hemisphere), with a major emphasis on basic concepts from geography—resource distribution, spatial interaction, areal differentiation, global
interdependence. The history of areas should be provided in order to illustrate
changes through time. The aspirations and problems of developing nations
need to be stressed. Emphasis should be given to the many interconnections
that exist between places and people in the modern world. This not only
includes resources necessary to support technologically based societies but
cultural interconnections as well—arts, literature, communication, religion,
music, and sports.

The 6th and 7th grade programs should emphasize geographic knowledge
of the world and its people. Physical geography and place location should be
stressed, along with such other geographic concepts as *spatial interaction,
interdependence, resource development and use, international trade,* and *human
habitation* with its effects on the environment. As was indicated in the 6th grade
program, it is recommended that *at least* one semester of systematic study be
devoted to Latin America in either the 6th *or* 7th grade.

Grade 8—Building a Strong and Free Nation: The United States

The 9th grade program is the study of the "epic of America," the development of the United States as a strong and free nation. The primary emphasis at
this level should be the social history and economic development of the

country, including cultural and aesthetic dimensions of the American experience. Attention should be given to the history of ordinary people doing ordinary things to include family life, work, leisure, and medical care. The unique contribution of the men and women who built the heritage we share should be stressed. The presentation must be realistic and exciting to the early adolescent. This program should stress the important role played by the United States in global affairs and the need to secure peaceful relations with all nations.

(*Note*: Most students today complete high school and, therefore, take a full year of U.S. history in the 11th grade. Consequently, some school districts have adopted course options at the 8th grade level. See the chart below.)

Grade 9—Systems that Make a Democratic Society Work: Law, Justice, and Economics

The 9th grade program focuses on the concepts *social stability* and *social change* and calls for one semester of study of the law and justice systems and one semester of economics. A functional knowledge of the law and justice systems, as well as a knowledge of the economic system—along with related skills and attitudes—are critical to the practice of citizenship. These courses should address issues that capitalize on the real-life problems of students. They should also provide many opportunities for developing critical-thinking, problem-solving, and social-participation skills.

The 9th grade placement of this subject matter is critical in terms of the developmental needs of the early adolescent. Besides, some 9th graders will no longer be in school to take these courses as 12th graders. Problems of alienation and disengagement from law, justice, and economic systems are widespread among adolescents. Many are left with the feeling that they are powerless to cope with the forces that affect their lives. The integrated study of these systems, which make a democratic society work, *presented in ways that are perceived by young adolescents as meaningful to their lives*, should assist in helping young people develop a sense of needed efficacy in dealing with these systems.

(*Note*: In states where the study of state history and government is required by legislative mandate, basic concepts from law, justice, and economics can be incorporated in such a course.)

Grade 10—Origins of Major Cultures: A World History

The 10th grade program should focus on the history of the major cultures and societies of the contemporary world. The course stresses the diverse economic, political, religious, and social systems. Historical perspective should be provided on major world events and movements. Students should develop a knowledge of and an appreciation for the contributions of many cultures to the collective wisdom of the human race. The course should include attention to those historical differences among people that lead to conflict. The course is basically history and should help students learn the skills and tools of historical analysis. Nonetheless, it incorporates related concepts from other social science disciplines, especially anthropology, geography, political science, and economics.

Grade 11—The Maturing of America: United States History

The 11th grade program should be a comprehensive course in American history that is organized chronologically and serves as a capstone for the study of American history in the elementary and secondary schools. The forces that shaped and continue to shape political, economic, and social institutions should be studied. Changes in social and cultural values should also be included. The effects of growing international involvements and commitments must be stressed. The growth of the arts and literature, social reform movements, the extension of civil rights, the labor movement, and the growth of government should be included. The diversity of ethnic and racial origins of Americans and the impact of this diversity on the development of the nation should be emphasized.

Grade 12—One-year course or courses required; selection(s) to be made from the following:

Issues and Problems of Modern Society

Issues and problems of modern society should provide numerous opportunities for students to make a critical analysis of enduring social issues. The scope is broadened to emphasize the global dimensions of American problems and issues.

Introduction to the Social Sciences

The introduction to the social sciences should deal with the content and modes of inquiry of the social sciences.

The Arts in Human Societies

The arts in human societies should allow students to learn about the cultures of the world through the arts and literature.

International Area Studies

As an in-depth cross-cultural study of selected areas of the world, the course focuses on the interaction of different cultures in a defined area of the world.

Social Science Elective Courses

Anthropology, Economics, Government, Psychology, Sociology *Supervised Experience in Community Affairs*

Figure A1. Optional Sequences for Grades 6–12

All the following options include:

1. One year of American history at grade 11.
2. Systematic study of all major culture regions of the world
3. At least one semester of economics and one semester of law-related studies

Local school districts may develop a mix-and-match option to capitalize on local teacher strengths, availability of instructional materials, and community expectations. Such locally developed sequences should, however, include the three components listed in 1, 2, and 3 above.

	Grade 6	Grade 7	Grade 8	Grade 9	Grade 10	Grade 11	Grade 12
Option 1	People and cultures: Representatives world regions	A changing world of many nations: A global view	U.S. history with emphasis on social history and economic development	Economics and law-related studies (one semester each)	World history (both Western and non-Western)	U.S. history (chronological, political, social, economic)	Series of options: see page 382 for list of possibilities
Option 2	European cultures with their extension into the Western Hemisphere	A changing world of many nations: A global view	Economics and law-related studies (one semester each)	Cultures of the non-Western world	The Western heritage	U.S. history (chronological, political, social, economic)	Government (one semester); Issues and problems of modern society (one semester)
Option 3	Land and people of Latin America	People and cultures: Representative world regions	Interdisciplinary study of the local region (geographic, social, economic, historical) with an environmental emphasis	World history and cultures (2-year sequence)		U.S. history (chronological, political, social, economic)	Economics and law-related studies (one semester each)
Option 4	People and cultures: Representative world regions	A changing world of many nations: A global view	Interdisciplinary study of the local region (geographic, social, economic, historical) with an environmental emphasis	World cultures	The Western heritage	U.S. history (chronological, political, social, economic)	Economics and law-related studies (one semester each)

Appendix 2

Designing a Social Studies Scope and Sequence for the 21st Century

Excerpted from H. Michael Hartoonian and Margaret A. Laughlin.
"Designing a Social Studies Scope and Sequence for the 21st Century."
Social Education (October 1989): 388-398. Reprinted with permission.

Goals

Social studies content is concerned with developing reflective, democratic citizenship within a global context and includes the disciplines typically classified as belonging to the social and behavioral sciences as well as history, geography, and content selected from law, philosophy, humanities, and mathematics. It also includes those topics and issues that focus on social problems, issues, and controversies. The social studies can be oriented to one discipline or multiple disciplines, depending upon the topic selected for study. Social studies programs address four educational goals:

• The development of enlightened democratic citizenship for effective participation in local, state, national, and international affairs
• The appreciation and understanding of our cultural heritage, including diversity and its role in contemporary society
• The acquisition of academic knowledge and abilities related to the study of the motives, actions, and consequences of human beings as they live individually as well as in groups and societies in a variety of place and time settings; and the joy of learning about self, others, and human history

• Learning "how to learn"—how to use prior knowledge to understand complex ideas and how to create new ideas

All these goals are of equal importance, for they reinforce each other. Thus the goal of citizenship is supported by the goals of discipline, academic study, and ongoing learning.

Program Scope: Major Curriculum Themes

The particular curriculum design suggested here is based upon ten themes that extend logically from the previously identified goals. These themes are included at each grade level with increasing sophistication and constitute, in large measure, the program scope. The themes help define the program's scope to the extent that they present perspectives that provide students the temporal, spatial, and cultural criteria necessary for comprehension and rational action. To some degree, any delineation of major themes is arbitrary. Whereas different themes may be emphasized at various grade levels, they should be included at every grade and may be presented in any coherent order based on the maturity level and ability of the students.

With the above in mind, examine Figure A2.

**Fig. A2 Major Scope
and Curriculum Themes**

SCOPE

Grade Levels

K   2 3 4 5 6 7 8 9 10 11 12

| ← Cultural Heritage → |
| ← Global Perspective → |
| ← Political/Economic → |
| ← Tradition and Change → |
| ← Social History → |
| ← Spatial Relationships → |
| ← Social Contracts → |
| ← Technology → |
| ← Peace/Interdependence → |
| ← Citizenship → |

Social Studies and Higher-Order Thinking

Social studies content and higher-order thinking are seen here in two different but *interrelated* ways. First, social studies content is viewed as a story about continuity and change over time—an exciting narrative or analytical study about people, events, and issues (Danto 1965). Second, social studies may be understood as a disciplined study or inquiry involving the creation, structuring, and use of knowledge (Bragaw and Hartoonian 1988). Thinking within the social studies curriculum should address both these ideas. Thus, social studies may be both an artful narrative *and* a set of assumptions, concepts, explanations, and biases that reflect the attitudes and craft of the community of scholars, including students and teachers, who construct social knowledge. A closer look at thinking in the social studies disciplines (history, geography, the social and behavioral sciences, and, in some cases, the humanities) reveals the use of concepts such as narrative, change, continuity, chronology, cause-and-effect relationships, evidence, and frame of reference. In other words, history and the social sciences can be defined as recorded narratives or stories about the past or present that describe change and continuity over time and seek to explain change and continuity through a series of cause-and-effect propositions based on evidence and shaped by the scholar's social frame of reference. We all attempt to find out not only what happened but why it happened, what trends can be suggested, and how and why humans behave in certain ways in different social settings. Some of the most important questions we consider when thinking about the past, present, and future of the social world include:

• How can we best conceptualize a topic, issue, theme, event, or behavior?

• What defines a historical period? What defines a theme? What defines an issue?

• What constitutes primary and secondary evidence? How can such evidence be evaluated and used? What evidence is missing?

• How are cause-and-effect relationships handled in a narrative or discourse?

The dynamic use of these questions and the concepts they embrace are fundamental to the way in which we conduct social inquiry. That is, the way in which we think about and with social knowledge is directly related to the concepts and questions we use and their relationship to one another. In social studies, as in most other fields of inquiry, there are several basic interrelated components of critical study involved in the construction and use of knowledge. They constitute the necessary elements in thinking about personal and social questions, and present a model for higher-order or reflective thinking. These components are identified here as (1) comprehension or conceptualization, (2) causality, (3) validity of explanation, and (4) creative extension.

The first or most fundamental level of study is for students to *conceptualize* the people, setting, story, or context of the phenomenon they are studying. At this level, the following questions are asked: What is going on? How have things changed? And, how have they remained the same? These kinds of questions help define the temporal and spatial context necessary for comprehending the issue, problem, topic, or theme studied. *Comprehension* also includes the knowledge and skills that students bring to the inquiry. What factual knowledge of major social or historical movements and cultures and what knowledge of the content and methods of the social sciences disciplines do the students have? As part of the process of comprehension, students must understand data in textual, visual, and quantitative form so as to be able to relate new contexts to previously learned data and knowledge, and to identify problems or issues.

The second level of study deals with *causality*. Once students conceptualize and comprehend the setting of the inquiry, they must then ask how and why the setting acquired its characteristics. Their inquiry should allow them to formulate cause and effect relationships and use logic in their own explanations of social and historical developments and to look for logic in the explanations of others. Specifically, students must use skills of analysis to help them gain some understanding of how to approach the problem of change over time and to recognize and explain major events, trends, or issues.

At the third level, students inquire into the accuracy of *validity* of the explanations suggested previously. Here students investigate bias, the nature of evidence, and the methods of evaluation used to validate explanations. To do this, students must have some familiarity with the techniques of quantitative and nonquantitative analysis as well as the ability to deal with diverse interpretations of data and to think critically about conflicting interpretations.

Finally, the fourth level of study is concerned with *creative extensions;* that is, students' creative inquiry into new settings and issues. Creativity and independent study abilities and skills are paramount at this level as students seek to combine insight and experience with logic to gain new knowledge. Here students begin to develop their own interpretations by establishing linkages and seeing connections between different historical or contemporary events and probing issues of causation and outcome. They also expand their use of knowledge by linking the past with the present and exploring the historical developments underlying present similarities and differences among the world's peoples. In sum, this fourth level interrelates with all other levels, thus creating the dynamics of what we understand as the conduct of inquiry and the nature of critical discourse.

Once again, it should be noted that neither the four components of study (comprehension and conceptualization, causality, validity of explanation, and creative extension) nor their related skills and abilities are mutually exclusive. The components do, however, suggest activities in which students should be engaged if they are to understand social inquiry. These activities are crucial for equipping students with the ability to communicate (listen, speak, discuss, and write) not only about interesting historical and contemporary social issues but also about the quality and accuracy of social inquiry itself. These skills with varying degrees of sophistication can be used throughout the social studies curriculum.

Appendix 3
Social Studies Within A Global Education

Excerpted from Willard M. Kniep. "Social Studies Within A Global Education." *Social Education* (October 1989): 399-403. Reprinted with permission.

Scope and Sequence

The scope of the curriculum should not be limited by tradition or by familiar topics that have always been taught. The determinants should be the purposes that we have set out for social studies, our best analysis of the current realities in which students live, the requirements of citizenship in the 21st century, and an understanding of the basic nature and elements of those realities from the scholarship of history, social science, and other disciplines.

The scope of the social studies curriculum, then, should reflect the present and historical realities of a global society. As a way to bring some order to thinking about those realities, I propose four essential elements of study in a global education that set the boundaries for the scope of the social studies curriculum.

1. The Study of Systems—including the *economic, political, ecological,* and *technological* systems dominating our interdependent world.

2. The Study of Human Values—both *universal values* defining what it means to be human and *diverse values* derived from group membership and contributing to unique worldviews.

3. The Study of Persistent Issues and Problems—including *peace* and *security*, national and international *development* issues, local and global *environmental* issues, and *human rights* issues.

4. The Study of Global History—focusing on the evolution of universal and diverse human values, the historical development of contemporary global systems, and the antecedent conditions and causes of today's global issues.

In organizing the sequence of the social studies curriculum, every effort should be made to retain the holistic character of global education. Doing so will ensure that students can capture the sense of interdependence characterizing the modern world. Furthermore, the sequence of study should lead to broad and transferable conceptual understanding of patterns and relationships. It must keep students at the center of their learning and their world.

As a way of achieving consistency with these principles, I propose using themes as basic organizers for the social studies curriculum. In the social studies curriculum, themes function as a means for focusing attention, for making connections among disparate elements across curriculums, and for applying what is learned to the rest of life.

This thematic model uses three types of themes for curriculum organization derived from the structural elements of the disciplines underlying the social studies. Each discipline uses *concepts* for organizing inquiry and for describing its structure and view of reality. Each studies certain *phenomena* that delimit its field of inquiry. Each focuses on *persistent problems* for which its knowledge may provide explanations or solutions.

Conceptual Themes

Work within social studies should be organized, first of all, around concepts: the big ideas forming the mental structures and language that human beings use for thinking about and describing the world. The particular concepts used as curricular themes are characteristically abstract and relational. They are not labels for real, concrete things, but generally describe how people, things, and events relate to one another. Such concepts, while shared in people's language and thinking about the world, are idiosyncratic to an extent since they are individually formed and reflect the transaction between persons' prior knowledge and experience and the meaning taken from new experience.

The five conceptual themes, listed and defined in the accompanying box, have been selected as basic curriculum organizers because they are essential to the development of a global perspective. They are metaconcepts in the sense that they consistently appear in the language and thinking of the social and natural sciences and because they serve as organizers around which other concepts tend to cluster.

120

Conceptual Themes for the Social Studies

1. Interdependence

We live in a world of systems in which the actors and components interact to make up a unified, functioning whole.

Related concepts: causation, community, exchange, government, groups, interaction systems.

2. Change

The process of movement from one state of being to another is a universal aspect of the planet and is an inevitable part of life and living.

Related concepts: adaption, cause and effect, development, evolution, growth, revolution, time.

3. Culture

People create social environments and systems comprised of unique beliefs, values, traditions, language, customs, technology, and institutions as a way of meeting basic human needs; shaped by their own physical environments and contact with other cultures.

Related concepts: adaption, aesthetics, diversity, languages, norms, roles, values, space-time.

4. Scarcity

An imbalance exists between relatively unlimited wants and limited available resources necessitating the creation of systems for deciding how resources are to be distributed.

Related concepts: conflict, exploration, migration, opportunity cost, policy, resources, specialization.

5. Conflict

People and nations often have differing values and opposing goals resulting in disagreement, tensions, and sometimes violence necessitating skill in coexistence, negotiation, living with ambiguity and conflict resolution.

Related concepts: authority, collaboration, competition, interests/positions, justice, power, rights.

Phenomenological Themes

Topical organization of textbooks and curriculums focused on phenomena—people, places, and events—is common in social studies. One of the problems with this approach has been that, by focusing on a single phenomenon such as a nation or region, we may overemphasize uniqueness and differences and ignore similarities and interconnectedness—an outcome that runs directly counter to developing a global perspective. In a global education, phenomenological themes would be selected for their contribution to understanding the world's systems, cultures, and historical evolution.

Phenomenological themes fall in two categories. The first is the *actors and components* playing major roles in the world's systems or within the sphere of human cultures and values. Actors meeting these criteria include specific nations, organizations, religious and cultural groups, significant individuals, and institutions. Components include geographic regions, significant documents, geological features, landforms, and systems and subsystems.

The second category of phenomenological themes is comprised of major *events*. Such events, both historical and contemporary, are selected because of their contribution to the development of contemporary world systems and the evolution of diversity and commonality of human values and cultures.

Specific phenomena are chosen as themes because we are convinced they are essential to students' understanding of the world. Individual choices depend, to a large extent, on the needs and location of students. For students in the United States, knowing the history, roles, and values of their own community, state, and nation is critical to understanding the world's systems and the interaction and evolution of cultures and values. So too, their historical perspective must include the major events in the development of their own country. At the same time, however, students will truly understand the world in which they live only if our choices include the broad range of actors, components, and events that continue to shape the systems, values, and history of our diverse planet.

Persistent Problem Themes

These themes embrace the global issues and problems characterizing the modern world. By engaging with persistent problems, students can clearly see their interdependent nature and how a variety of actors, themselves included, affect the problems and their solutions. The study of persistent problems would be incomplete unless it contributed to an understanding of their historical antecedents and the ways in which problems and their solutions relate to cultural perspectives and human values.

It is possible to generate a lengthy list of specific persistent problems that plague us globally and locally. However, the vast majority of problems seem to fall into the following four categories.

Peace and Security	**National/International Development**
the arms race	hunger and poverty
East-West relations	overpopulation
terrorism	North-South relations
colonialism	appropriate technology
democracy vs. tyranny	international debt crisis

Environmental Problems
acid rain
pollution of streams
depletion of rain forests
nuclear-waste disposal
maintenance of fisheries

Human Rights
apartheid
indigenous homelands
political imprisonment
religious persecution
refugees

Persistent problems, by their very nature, permeate every level of existence—from global to national to local—with their symptoms and causes. Moreover, the solutions to persistent problems will come both through individual behaviors taken collectively and through policy decisions taken multilaterally. Because of this, themes in this category consistently provide opportunities for students to find their role as citizens and develop their abilities for social participation in local versions of global problems or local efforts to alleviate global problems.

1991 ASCD Networks for Social Studies Educators

ASCD sponsors numerous networks that enable members to exchange ideas, share common interests, identify and solve problems, grow professionally, and establish collegial relationships. Several may be of particular interest to readers of this book:

Social Issues and Education

Facilitator: James T. Sears, Professor, University of South Carolina, Wardlaw 230, Columbia, SC 29208. Telephone: (803) 777-6003.

Interdisciplinary Curriculum

Facilitator: Benjamin P. Ebersole, Hershey Public Schools, Box 898, Hershey, PA 17033. Telephone: (717) 534-2501, ext. 252.

Authentic Assessment Network

Facilitator: Albert N. Koshiyama, Administrator, Local Evaluation Assistance, California Department of Education, 721 Capitol Mall, Sacramento, CA 95814. Telephone: (916) 324-7147.

For more information on these and other current ASCD networks, call ASCD's Field Services Department at (703) 549-9110, ext. 506 or 502. Or write to ASCD at 1250 N. Pitt Street, Alexandria, VA 22314.